G000231708

At Arnotts of Dublin

At Arnotts of Dublin
1843–1993

Ronald Nesbitt

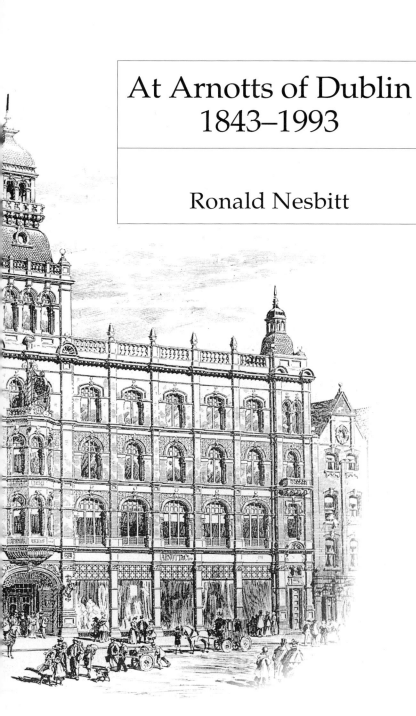

First published in 1993 by
A. & A. Farmar
Beech House
78 Ranelagh Village
Dublin 6

© Ronald Nesbitt 1993

ISBN 0 9509295 4 9

All illustrations, unless otherwise stated, are from Arnotts' archives

All rights reserved. No part of this book may be reprinted or
reproduced or utilized in electronic, mechanical or other means, now
known or hereafter invented, including photocopying and recording, or
any information storage or retrieval system, without permission in
writing from the publishers.

British Library Cataloguing in Publication Data
A CIP catalogue record for this book is available from the British Library

Typeset by Phototype-Set Ltd.
Printed by Criterion Press
Historical and picture research by Peter Costello
Index by Helen Litton
Cover design by Syd Bluett
Cover photograph by Image Now Consultants

*To the staff of Arnotts
past and present
whose own dedication
has made Arnotts what it is*

CONTENTS

FOREWORD

IT GIVES ME much pleasure to write a few words of introduction to Ronald Nesbitt's history of Arnotts, which coincides with the company's celebration of one hundred and fifty years in business.

Arnotts derives its name from Sir John Arnott who was a most important businessman in the mid-1800s, having served as a Member of Parliament and three terms as Lord Mayor of Cork. Sir John was involved in a considerable number of business ventures, including Cannocks of Limerick and *The Irish Times*.

From its formation in 1843 Arnotts progressed in business in a slow but steady manner, marred only by a disastrous fire in 1894. With commendable alacrity the directors of the day got business under way again and embarked upon a programme of reconstruction.

Since these early times Arnotts built up a major business by ability to anticipate and meet the needs and expectations of its customers. It became and indeed remains, a household name throughout Ireland.

Many will recollect that it was not until 1977 that the larger stores stayed open all day on Saturdays. Before that, they were closed for the afternoon when trade was potentially at its greatest. In the 1950s through to the 1970s the busiest days in the Dublin stores were 'Holy Days', or Church holidays, when large numbers flocked from provincial areas to shop in Dublin, usually by train to avail of cheap excursion tickets.

The Nesbitt influence in Arnotts began at the turn of the century with Alexander, who was succeeded by his son William, grandson Ronald and great-grandson Michael.

This is, by any standards, a most remarkable history of family dedication to the service of a company.

William Nesbitt was keen to support home industry and established a number of manufacturing units most of which were run as subsidiary companies of the parent. In their day, they were most successful and included units manufacturing hats, brassières, shirts, dresses and children's coats. Brassière and foundation garments were at one stage manufactured in association with Courtaulds and the enterprise constituted a sizeable business in its own right as, indeed, did the shirt manufacturing operation.

Until recent years the company had the greatest wholesale drapery enterprise in Ireland. It is worthy of mention that the company began wholesaling as far back as the 1850s.

The 1960s saw much activity in the company, including the purchase of Boyers' store in North Earl Street and significant rebuilding and alterations in Henry Street, coupled with the purchase of Wests' premises at 102 and 103 Grafton Street. Sizeable construction projects were put in hand at both Boyers and Wests. These developments paid handsome dividends magnified, to a significant degree, by a mini-boom in trading which had some of its roots in a major jump in incomes and rising inflation.

At this time, Arnotts had a number of noteworthy promotions. These were largely the brainchild of John Doody, a director with considerable talent and flair for marketing. Their significance was enhanced by the attendance of internationally known personalities. Without any doubt, these promotions were a great success and brought Arnotts' name to the forefront at that time.

Arnotts has also been in the vanguard of other aspects of business activity in this country. It was one of the first companies in the state to install a computer (1966). Shortly afterwards, it marketed instalment credit, by means of the credit-card system. The company has also been a leader in the field of pensions for staff. It is quite remarkable that its 'death in service' benefit dates back to 1883! The modern-day pension fund was initiated shortly before the Second

World War. Ronald Nesbitt, who always regarded staff relations as the quintessence of company policy, has played a key role in building up the contemporary staff pension fund.

Arnotts, despite a disastrous fire on its premises, two world wars, a rebellion, a civil war, market depressions and all the other negative factors that have afflicted Ireland, has continued to trade and has never failed to make a profit or been unable to pay a dividend to its shareholders. The company now faces one of the greatest challenges in its long history when it undertakes the changes that will be necessary to trade successfully in the twenty-first century. Arnotts has accepted the challenge and has prepared itself for what it perceives as the trading environment likely to develop in the years that lie ahead.

As one reads the chapters in this book, the full details of some aspects mentioned in this introduction unfold and make an entertaining and fascinating journey back in time.

Michael G. O'Connor
22 April 1993

INTRODUCTION

How long ago is that? Year Phil Gilligan died. . . . Six years. Ten years ago: ninetyfour he died, yes that's right, the big fire at Arnott's. Val Dillon was lord mayor.

James Joyce *Ulysses*

THE HISTORY OF A successful department store such as Arnotts is not normally dramatic. It has been so far a story of five generations of men and women, and indeed of families, working in groups called departments. There have been relatively larger numbers in Arnotts than in many other stores because our staff aims to sell and selling cannot be automated. In addition, machinery for sales accounting has only in recent times become sophisticated enough to take over much of the daily office grind.

The documents on which this story is based reflect that humdrum routine; early minutes of the weekly meetings of directors are laconic to the point of boredom, beautifully inscribed, without a spelling mistake, but lacking colour. No event of wider importance is mentioned, not even the beginnings or endings of the two world wars, and the Rising of 1916 is noted only because a wholesale customer had not paid his account as promised 'owing to the recent rebellion'. So the colour in Arnotts' story is provided by the people involved themselves and by the goods they sell.

But one event lights vividly our view of Arnotts past – the disastrous fire of 1894. On the night of 4 May, the houses numbered 11 to 15 Henry Street and the buildings on the areas behind numbers 9 to 17 Henry Street and back to Prince's Street, which had been developed together since the beginning of trading in 1843 to make the department store, were totally destroyed.

The fire produced a flurry of action which is reflected in the record of directors' meetings. Its financial effects were not cleared until well into the 1900s. The fire also destroyed some of our records including Book No. 4 of minutes of directors' meetings dating from the registration of the private limited company in 1871. Book No. 1, for the period 1871 to 1878, is also missing, but Books Nos. 2 and 3, covering the years 1878 to 1890, survive leaving a gap between the latter date and 1894.

So Arnotts' story from 1843 to 1877 has to be reconstructed from public records, but for three small, bound books and a montage of photographs compiled by Henry Beater, Arnotts' company secretary from 1887 to 1933. Even the memory of Alexander Nesbitt, who entered Arnotts in 1867 at the age of sixteen, was not tapped in time to record much. Most of what is known from him came through stories retold by his son, William.

One of the three books, bound in black leather, stamped in gold 'Chairman's Private Figures', records sales figures from 1856. The second contains the partnership and private company account from 1863 to 1876. The third, with striped cover, contains directors' reports and balance sheets and, more informatively, notes verbatim of proceedings at the annual general meetings from 1876 to 1909. The striped book provides occasional flashbacks to the earliest period.

We have attendance books of the general meetings of shareholders from 1876 and, thanks to Henry Beater, company secretary up to 1933, and his successors to date, a fairly full archive. One aim of this book is to summarise this material and to encourage its preservation.

The author is indebted to Frances Tuomey for information about George Cannock, Andrew White and John Arnott, the result of her research for a monograph on the early history of the Limerick department store, Cannock & Co., in which Arnott, as well as Cannock, was interested.

The reader will detect indebtedness to many members of staff in the text, but quite undetectable, he hopes, is the work in Arnotts of Gillian Muldoon and Siobhán Meehan in deciphering for word-processor what the author fondly imagined was his clear sloping script. Maeve Kenny's enthusiastic marshalling of material for illustration must also be commended; also the patience of my wife Ella who was deprived of the dining-room table for a couple of years; and not forgotten Tony and Anna Farmars' enthusiastic editing and production of this book; Anna's careful work on the text, including rewriting and pruning where necessary, can hardly be over-estimated.

George Cannock shortly before his death in 1876

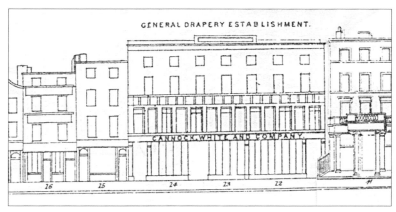

Facade of Cannock & White, Henry Street, in the 1850s (*Shaw's Directory*)

1 THE EARLY YEARS OF THE DEPARTMENT STORE 1843–1875

THE YEAR 1843, just two years before the height of the Famine, might not seem to have been a good time for George Cannock and Andrew White to sell their business as wholesale woollen and linen drapers in Washington Street, Cork and start trading in partnership in number 14 Henry Street, Dublin. But the disaster of the Famine had been developing over the previous twenty years, particularly in the west and south-west of Ireland, and Dublin was further away from its economic effects than Cork. The city's population was some 250,000 out of over eight million in the whole country.

In addition, the expanding industrial production of neighbouring Britain and Europe was creating the goods for trading on which the growth of shops such as that of Cannock & White into department stores could be based. So it turned out to be a good year – so good, in fact, that the need for money to finance the growing business was almost immediate.

In 1845 Andrew Reid and his son, Patrick, who were bankers, lent £6,000 on debenture to the business and number 13 Henry Street was added to number 14. After the death of Andrew White in early 1848, the Reids were joined by John Arnott who also invested £6,000. He rather surprisingly bought the lease of number 16 Henry Street, the front part of which was never occupied by the business.

The acquisition of scattered houses now looks like a scramble to buy property in the centre of Henry Street with the development of a large business in mind. The leases of these properties and others, and in recent years the freeholds of all of them, have been held by Arnotts, but trading in 1848 was concentrated in numbers 13 and 14 under the name 'Cannock White & Co., General drapers'.

Henry Street, built about 1760, was never a 'good' residential street and rapidly became a street of mixed business. It was in the usual Georgian pattern of basement and several storeys on the street with long, narrow gardens behind, completed by two-storey coach houses at the back.

But with the continued line of Mary Street, Earl Street and Talbot Street it was the narrowest of the thoroughfares radiating from the old centre of Dublin above Parliament Street, down Capel Street and out across the north-eastern quarter of the Georgian city.

In addition, Henry Street was placed centrally to the splendid width of Sackville Street (now O'Connell Street). Narrow streets make good shopping streets and Henry Street was destined to become a centre of shopping in Dublin.

A map of Dublin about 1825 shows its north-east quarter up to the North Circular Road already in place. An 1821 engraving, after George Petrie, of Sackville Street, complete with the General Post Office and Nelson's Pillar, looks recognisable as today's O'Connell Street from what was Carlisle Bridge (replaced by the greater width of O'Connell Bridge in 1880), give or take modern traffic, Nelson's Pillar and the dress of the men and women.

Little is known of the detail of the early trade in Cannock & White. In the *Dublin Almanac and Directory* (the predecessor of Thom's) it was called 'General drapery and haberdashery' in numbers 12, 13 and 14 Henry Street. In 1855, 'House furnishing' was added. There is a record of sales from 1856, which totalled in that year £276,611 – a figure at the lower end of a range around £300,000 (about £20 million in 1990 terms) which continued until the end of the century. By 1858, numbers 11 and 15 had also been occupied and the description became, a little more exotically, 'General drapers and house furnishers and importers of Berlin wool and embroidery'. In 1865 the business was renamed Arnott, John & Co. The description 'General drapers and house furnishers' in the Dublin directories continued through the years of registration of the private limited company in 1871 to the 1875 flotation of the public limited Arnott & Co. (The word 'Dublin' was added later.)

John Arnott was a Scot from Aughermuchty near Glasgow. Born in 1814, he moved to Cork at the age of twenty to work in a small store. Later he traded in Belfast and Glasgow with his brother-in-law. (These shops with the name 'Arnott' never had any other link with Arnotts of Dublin.) In the late 1840s Arnott returned to Cork and opened a large drapery store in Patrick Street. He developed as a courageous and largely successful Victorian entrepreneur and a popular philanthropist. He spread his interests into flour-milling, baking, brewing, ship-building and manufacturing, became Deputy Lieutenant of County Cork, Chairman of the Cork and Macroom railway, chief proprietor of *The Irish Times* and of the Bristol Steam Navigation Co. He was Lord Mayor of Cork from 1859 to 1861, was knighted by the Lord Lieutenant in 1859 at the opening of the new St Patrick's Street Bridge and represented Kinsale in Parliament as a Liberal.

John Arnott must have held George Cannock in high regard for he not only invested in his Henry Street venture but also in 1850 joined Cannock in taking over the drapery business in Limerick that was to develop as Cannock & Co. As for George Cannock, he concentrated his energy on managing Cannock White & Co. of Henry Street and visited Limerick only occasionally. He lived over the shop in Henry Street with his housekeeper, by whom he had two daughters. In 1865 he retired to live in London and, as we have seen, the business was renamed Arnott & Co.

The main reason for Arnotts going public is thought to have been Sir John Arnott's need for cash because of the failure of some of his other enterprises. He was so venturesome that would not be surprising. In 1865, his stake in the business was £58,000 compared with the two Reids' £35,000, whereas in 1876 it was less than £15,000 and Patrick Reid's was over £54,000.

But another reason surely was the flexibility provided by the recent legalisation of limited liability. It is significant

Facade of Arnott & Co. in the 1870s

John Arnott as a public figure; here he is being chaired through Cork on the completion of his three years Mayoralty (*Illustrated London News* 18 January 1862)

that in *Thom's Directory* of 1888 the description of the business is given as 'Wholesale and retail drapers, upholsterers and cabinet makers, carpet, curtain and general warehousemen'; this style, chosen naturally by Arnotts' management, is definitely more ambitious, showing an established confidence. We shall see later that it followed the occupation of extra space behind Henry Street.

The move into wholesaling seems to have developed early, in the 1850s. In the year 1859, total sales were just £300,000, in 1862 they dropped sharply to £226,000, and by 1872 they rebounded to £322,000; in 1895, when separate figures for the two trading divisions are first available, sales were £284,000 (retail £132,000, wholesale £152,000). Without a similar contribution from wholesale sales from the 1850s these total sales could not have been achieved. One of the earliest members of staff, Daniel Creedon, who joined in 1844, was called 'wholesale managing director' in a general meeting of 1879. Creedon had been company secretary until 1876 when he was elected a director. At the same meeting, William Freeman was referred to as 'retail managing director'; he also had entered the business in 1844 and became a director in 1876.

It seems reasonable to guess that by the late 1850s, after all five houses from 11 to 15 Henry Street had been occupied and the full scope of the retail trade delineated, the energies of some of the cloth and clothing buyers would spill over into trade with other retailers, shops mostly outside Dublin, whose buyers would be drawn to Dublin for supplies and ideas. Certainly, there was a strong trade with Cannocks of Limerick.

Wholesale trade developed in the same way in Todd Burns of Mary Street and most notably in Pim Brothers of South Great Georges Street, who were considered to be the most successful wholesalers in the drapery trade until they abandoned wholesaling after the First World War. With Arnotts, these three businesses were called 'the dual houses'. To judge by Arnotts, the buyers (trading managers) ran twin departments, without any separation of trading accounts. The retail section of the department was situated on the ground or other easily accessible floor and the whole-

Two early partners: (left) C. Murray (right) William McNaught

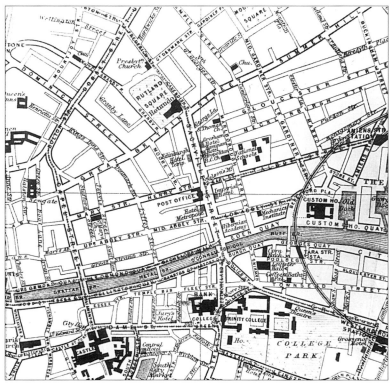

Maps of the Henry Street district in Victorian times (*Thorough Guide to Ireland* 1892)

sale section anywhere, including basement or upper floor, that space could be found.

This was considered an economical use of space in a multi-storey building. Rents today illustrate the high value of space on street or other ground floor level compared with the lower values of upper floors, despite lifts and escalators. But profits on upper floors helped to cover fixed expenses, and in the retail department store upper floors housed departments that customers were willing to seek out, particularly those that required a lot of space.

The population of Dublin City (between the Royal and Grand canals) had risen steadily in the thirty years up to 1850. After that it increased very little until about 1900. But the suburban townships on the south side of Dublin, where many of Arnotts' customers lived, continued to grow. By the 1870s nearly a quarter of the Dublin population lived in these self-governing areas. The development of the railway system helped country-wide trading. Broadstone Station was built from 1841 onwards and Kingsbridge (Heuston) Station from 1845. The line to Cork was completed in 1849, to Galway in 1851, to Belfast in 1855, to Tralee in 1859, to Derry in 1861, to Sligo in 1862 and to Wexford as late as 1872. Thus provincial shops could rapidly adopt the latest fashions to the benefit of themselves and the wholesalers in Dublin.

This growth was not achieved without competition and setbacks due to poor economic conditions; the earliest reports of speeches by chairmen of Arnotts invariably refer to weather conditions and the state of agriculture.

More is known about Arnotts' early people than their trading, due particularly to the splendid photographic montage made in 1907 by the company secretary, Henry Beater. George Cannock has, like John Arnott, a strong self-assured look. His bewhiskered face without moustache dates him as he was, an older man founding a business with younger men such as William McNaught and Orlando Beater who joined him in 1843, and C. Murray, Daniel Creedon and William Freeman who joined him in 1844. John Arnott was more than half a generation younger than Cannock.

In 1864 Murray, who had been woollens buyer, was promoted to manager, probably wholesale manager because
the name 'woollens' has since been traditionally a wholesale department. He died four years later; presumably that
was the date of the appointment of Daniel Creedon in his
place. Murray certainly looks the most old-fashioned of the
group. All the oldest are marked by hair round their faces
in sideburns or fringes, with cleanshaven cheeks and lips.
As the century passed, full-bearded faces became the
fashion but generally more tidily controlled; this was, of
course, the century in which men became progressively
quieter in their dress.

Patrick Reid was, with John Arnott, the main financial
backer of the business from the beginning to 1886. Arnott
was usually absent, but Reid was there continuously. It is
perhaps eloquent of his modesty, or discretion as a banker,
that no photograph of him appears in Beater's display, and
that he allowed Arnott to give his name to the company
when Cannock departed in 1865.

2 ARNOTTS TO THE FIRE 1876–1894

THE FIRST HALF-YEARLY general meeting of share-holders of the new public limited company was held on Friday, 1 September 1876. This was the eleventh half-yearly meeting since the registration in 1871 of the private limited company. There is no record of the preceding ten general meetings.

Surprisingly, Sir John Arnott did not attend this first meeting, nor indeed did he attend any other such meeting until those held during the six weeks after the fire in 1894. This was probably his usual behaviour in the years before 1876, though he had bought *The Irish Times* in 1873 and had many other interests in Dublin to bring him to the city. He had served his time in the drapery trade and his letters prove that he understood it thoroughly. He was, however, content to follow the progress of Arnotts from his base in Cork.

Patrick Reid, vice-chairman, presided; the other directors present were James F. Lombard, Orlando Beater, William Freeman (retail manager), Daniel Creedon (wholesale manager), with Elijah J. Hudson as secretary. Fashions in names change too! William McNaught's death, after service in Arnotts since the start of the business in 1843, was noted with regret.

The directors reported a very satisfactory half-year despite 'the general depression of trade' and the chairman added that sales had been £2–£3,000 (and profits, at 12½ per cent, a half per cent) above the average of the previous ten half-years. The net profit after charges was £10,598 of which the dividend at the rate of 12½ per cent a year absorbed £9,377.

Arnotts Directors of the early 1880s (from a photomontage of 1907)

Sir John Arnott   Orlando Beater

Daniel Creedon   William Freeman

James F. Lombard   Elijah J. Hudson

The size of the dividend surprised one of the younger men, Alexander Nesbitt, who was twenty-five years of age at the time, with a mere nine years' service. He complained, about the year 1900 and with the benefit of hindsight, that the directors in these early days were paying away in dividends the lifeblood of the business.

To complete the picture of Arnotts' first year as a public company the figures for the second six months of 1876, reported to shareholders at the twelfth general meeting of February 1877, must be added. The net profit was £13,500 making £24,098 for the year, and the dividend was at the same rate of 12½ per cent a year – this was stated to be 2 per cent a year more than had been paid for the previous autumn half-year, the last half-year of the private limited company.

The shareholders had been accustomed to steady trading in the boom of the early 1870s, which did not falter until 1878, and showed little hesitation in expressing their approval of generous dividends. The directors were as prudent as they could be otherwise; they wrote off £1,000 against debtors in each half-year of 1876, bringing the total for this vital figure down to £45,573. In the euphoria of a good six months' trading to July 1877, they provided another £2,000 to redeem debentures and £1,000 to add to the reserve fund. This report concluded that over 15 per cent had been earned on the ordinary capital over twelve months; that suggests a dividend cover of 1⅕ times. This would be thin in today's steady, even if moderated, inflation.

The goddess Nemesis appeared in the autumn of 1877 causing depression and 'extreme caution in the conduct of the wholesale trade'. Dividends were cut to 11⅖ per cent and six months later to 10 per cent. Dividends remained at 10 per cent until 1884 when they were reduced for the next ten years to 8⅛ per cent, with one 'blip' to 6¼ per cent. During this period to 1884 the directors continued to build the reserve fund up to £12,000 but, while profits grew thinner, debtors and creditors built up steadily on either side of the balance sheets. That of July 1883 (see page 20), gives an omnibus figure of a monstrous £256,709 covering

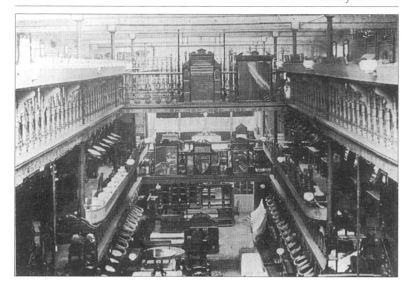

How the store looked before the fire: (above) sitting-room and bedroom furniture (below) curtains and window blinds

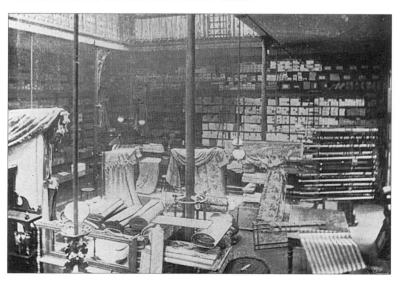

'premises, stock, goodwill, house and warehouse furniture, plant, etc., etc.' A significant proportion of this was an embarrassingly large figure for goodwill established when the original owners floated the company in 1875.

There were dissident shareholders; in 1878 William Molony, forbear of the family well-known in the drapery trade in this century, posed the robust question: 'How is it that a great and successful company like this should be paying 6 per cent on debentures?' (The yield on gilts at this time was just over 3 per cent.)

The reply came from James F. Lombard J.P.[1] 'It was upon the wealth of the chairman's father who came into the business thirty-three or thirty-four years ago that the concern prospered; at the time the limited company was formed he held a large amount of stock, and it was thought that 6 per cent was the proper price on its conversion into debentures.' The chairman, Patrick Reid, remarked that if the directors saw fit to reissue the debentures at 4½ per cent he would take any or all of them at this price. Orlando Beater said he would do the same for the parties he represented.

Molony did not return to this charge until September 1882, suggesting that 4 per cent was a proper rate for the debentures and, rather cunningly, that the 2 per cent difference might be put into a fund for the families of employees who might die in their service. Lombard again 'thought it right to say, in the absence of one gentleman [Patrick Reid] that when shareholders did not feel as anxious as now to take up the debentures this gentleman took £50,000 to £60,000 and he had an honest right to a preference'.

At the following general meeting, of March 1883, the chairman, Patrick Reid, presented a cheque for £250 to start the fund proposed by Molony. Thus ended the attack on the debenture front.

---

[1] This James Fitzgerald Lombard had developed, with Sir John Arnott, from 1872 onwards the area of houses off the South Circular Road (between Harrington Street and Clanbrassil Street) where Arnott Street and Lombard Street now stand as memorials to them.

Instead John Kennedy, a shareholder, asked in September 1883 for details of the large asset headed 'premises, stock, goodwill etc.' He was refused this information on the grounds that it was a trade secret. Returning to the attack, he complained, firstly, that the reserve was invested in the business and not in some outside asset such as Consols; he next queried the fact that only two of the directors were paid for their work. Apparently the others were content with the dividends on their quite small shareholdings and the managing directors' gratitude. Kennedy was not impressed. 'Gratitude', he snorted, 'is all humbug in a public company.'

Kennedy was right to ask for details of the assets, but was wrong about the reserve fund if he meant what Orlando Beater took him to mean. Suggesting payment for directors highlighted the undeveloped nature of arrangements in the early days of limited liability. But Kennedy's work bore fruit more quickly than most planting.

In March 1884, after announcing the thinnest half-year profits to date and a dividend cut to a rate of 8⅛ per cent per annum, the chairman called attention to a breakdown of the large item for assets. He also mentioned the resignation of James F. Lombard (probably because of other business interests) and the co-option of Samuel Smalldridge, a name not unknown in the printing industry. (See pages 20–21 for the balance sheets of July 1883 and January 1884 which clearly show the change.)

In the written account of the meeting of 1 March 1884 the chairman spoke of unexpected opposition, and warm weather diminishing the demand for winter goods (years later Arnotts was still being caught out by mild winters and cold summers). Only two questions were asked, by a shareholder named McClean, who evidently liked the sound of his own voice but did not always understand what he was saying. In the first he confused the dividend rate of 8⅛ per cent with the return he was getting having paid £6 on the market for the £4 share. In the other question, however, by asking why the stock-in-trade was 'taken by the heads of the departments', he certainly hit one nail squarely on the head. Reading between the lines it is obvious that the half-year had worried the directors considerably, and that crucial question in trading, the value of the unsold stocks, had come to the fore.

Orlando Beater said Mr Gardner (of the auditors Craig Gardner) 'had wished the buyers to sign the stocks . . . and if the shareholders knew the anxiety which the directors took in the affairs of the house, they would have the fullest confidence. The directors had now a good deal more of the assistance of Sir John Arnott. He, Sir John, would co-operate with them in carrying on this concern with still greater energy.'

Calling up the spirit of Sir John from the 'vasty deep' of Cork was, of course, to placate the shareholders; the directors were well able to run the business without him and normally had a firm grasp of the figures. Their very regularity hinted at careful 'management'.

Looking at the detail of assets suddenly revealed in the balance sheet of January 1884 it can be seen that the original figure for goodwill had been £146,673 and for premises a more reasonable £95,922, which had been written down to £67,000 and £90,000 respectively. The figure for total assets in 1884, omitting debtors and cash, was £230,254 compared with £256,709 a year previously, a difference of £26,454. The net profit for the half-year was a nicely tailored but scarcely believable £8,906. In view of the directors' agitation over stocks the figure of £65,008, which came down to £53,431 with a lower net profit of £6,749 six months later, must have caused the auditors some worry – no wonder the heads of departments were asked to sign their stock lists. It looks as if a very optimistic valuation of the stock had been accepted by the managing directors in January 1884 to soften the shock of revelation of items such as goodwill, but there was still an unexplained injection of £26,454, or more probably, allowing for exaggerated profits, a figure of over £30,000. The source of this unexplained injection emerged some years later, in March 1887.

From this time to the fire in 1894, premises remained at £90,000, with only £20,000 added in 1888 for leave to occupy part of numbers 9 and 10 Henry Street. But the unhappy figure of £67,000 for goodwill was merely nibbled away at £1,000 a year until in 1886 the 'reserve

BALANCE SHEET MADE UP TO 31ST JULY, 1883.

CAPITAL AND LIABILITIES.

	£	s.	d.
To Capital Account, 37,510 Shares £4 paid-up ...	150,040	0	0
Debentures	60,500	0	0
Sundry Trade & Cash Creditors ...	112,153	13	8
„ Reserve Fund Account	11,000	0	0

Profit and Loss:—

Balance from 31st Jan., 1883 £4,206 16 7

Net Profit for Half-year ending 31st July, 1883, after Payment of Salaries, Expenses of Management, Income Tax and all other Charges, Bad & Doubtful Debts, etc., £9,531 9s. 0d.

Less—

Interest on Debenture £1,571 11s. 3d., and carried to Reserve Fund £1,000 ... 6,959 17 9

	11,166	14	4
	£344,860	8	0

PROPERTY AND ASSETS.

	£	s.	d.
By Premises, Stock, Goodwill of Business, House and Warehouse Furniture, Plant, etc., etc., ...}	256,709	0	0
„ Sundry Debtors	71,087	16	4
„ Cash in Bank and Cash and Bills Receivable on Hands	17,063	12	8
	£344,860	8	0

After the shareholders' meeting of 1883, in which the customary reporting of two-thirds of assets as a single figure (see above) was criticised, the directors decided to reveal the constituents of the capital asset figure; the balance sheet for 1883-4 (right) shows how they did so.

BALANCE SHEET MADE UP TO 31ST JANUARY, 1884.

CAPITAL AND LIABILITIES.

	£	s.	d.
To Capital Account, 37,510 Shares £4 paid-up ...	150,040	0	0
" Liabilities—Debentures ... 60,500 0 0			
" Sundry Trade & Cash Creditors 78,805 7 10	139,305	7	10
" Reserve Fund Account	12,000	0	0
" PROFIT AND LOSS:—			
Balance from 31st July, 1883 £3 664 14 4			
Net Profit for Half - year ending 31st Jan., 1884, after Payment of Salaries, Expenses of Management, Income Tax and all other Charges, Bad & Doubtful Debts, etc., £8,906 4s. 7d.			
Less—			
Interest on Debenture £1,571 11s. 3d., and carried to Reserve Fund £1,000 ... 6,834 13 4	9,999	7	8
	£311,344	15	6

PROPERTY AND ASSETS.

			£	s.	d.
By Premises Account, Original Cost, ...	£95,922	0	0		
Less—Written off, from time to time, to this date ...	5,922	0	0	90,000	0 0
By Goodwill of Business, Original Cost	146,673	0	0		
Less—Written off, from time to time, to this date ...	79,673	0	0	67,000	0 0
By Plant, Furniture, and Fittings, Original Cost	16,853	0	0		
Less Written off from time to time, to this date ...	9,153	0	0	7,700	0 0
By Stock-in-Trade, taken by Heads of Departments	65,008	10	5		
By Horses, Vans, Household Provisions, etc.	546	8	6	65,554	18 11
Sundry Debtors				60,418	19 8
By Cash in Bank, and Cash and Bills Receivable on Hands				20,670	16 11
				£311,344	15 6

fund', by that time £12,000, was switched across the balance sheet to reduce goodwill to £53,000.

Further questions about the figures revealed in early 1884 came at the general meeting of August of that year from a solicitor called Adams. Robert Gardner, of Craig Gardner, answered that shareholders in the public company had certainly 'paid a large sum for goodwill'.

The directors of Arnotts never felt comfortable with the item goodwill; Patrick Reid declared it was their intention to continue to write it down, along with the figure for premises. In fact, the writing down of premises did not come effectively until Alexander Nesbitt took control and was really pressed forward by his son, William.

In 1884, and largely accounting for losses on trading, came the closure of a separate shop for house furnishing, ironwork, china and glass in number 50 Henry Street, bought and opened with a flourish in 1878. This was the first, but not the last, time Arnotts failed to produce the management needed for trading outside the main store. The chairman declared 'it would be utterly impossible for the managing directors to give it the requisite super-intendence'. That he did not use the word 'management' may tell us something about Patrick Reid.

Belonging to a banking family, he was wealthy and secure, most generous and modest; the reverse side of these qualities may have been some aloofness from the trading struggle leading to indecision. The investment of the reserve fund of £12,000 in two fixed-interest securities in 1885, one of the more foolish suggestions of shareholder McClean, showed a lack of touch; it was rapidly reversed since it yielded less than 4 per cent – reversed moreover at a slight loss of capital. But this mistake can well be blamed on Patrick Reid's advisors for he died in autumn 1886, as also did William Freeman. His brother John Hamilton Reid[2] and William Molony were co-opted in their places.

At the general meeting of March 1887, with John Hamilton Reid in the chair, Orlando Beater revealed that in

---

[2]The name will be recognised as that of a forebear of Miss Hamilton Reid who was until quite recently lady chairman of Switzer & Co.

1884 there had been 'resignation of directors and so forth and Mr Patrick Reid then Chairman acted in a way that he (Mr Beater) never knew the like of in a case of the kind. Of his own volition he made the concern a present of £30,000.'

Here is the answer to the unexplained improvement in the balance sheet of January 1884. The £30,000, which must be thought of as approaching £2 million in 1993, was a magnificent gift. Patrick Reid may have felt unease at continuing to draw 6 per cent on the debentures of which he and Sir John Arnott held the bulk, when the appropriate rate had dropped to nearer 4 per cent. He may also have been embarrassed at the revelation in 1884 of the enormous price at which the goodwill had been sold to the shareholders ten years earlier. But the gift, as an address to him from his fellow directors stated, 'was the more enhanced by the fact that it had been privately given. An act so princely exhibits faithfully the unostentatious nobility and generosity of the donor.' Bravo, for once, Victorian rhetoric!

With Patrick Reid's death passed one of the men who dominated this period. The other, always in the background, was Sir John Arnott. Despite a tactful invitation to contribute he did not follow Reid's example. He usually wrote letters or sent messages. In February of 1886 he asked a shareholder, James Carlyle, to announce at a meeting that he had noticed a report in a Dublin paper about the appointment of another director. He, Sir John, did not think another director was needed but 'if his brother directors and shareholders thought that another was required, it would only be in keeping with goodwill and with fairness that the director should be a Catholic gentleman (hear, hear) considering that the great majority of the people in Ireland are of that faith'. William Freeman then remarked at length that it was unnecessary to import the word religion into the affairs of the company, also to applause. The loquacious McClean remarked that Sir John was a big man in the country but he had made a mistake in this (bringing religion into it).

Sir John was probably thinking of William Molony who was co-opted in autumn 1886. He was also a director of the

ARNOTT & CO., DUBLIN, LTD.

THE SALE COMMENCES TO-DAY
OF THE VALUABLE STOCK OF

Mr. J. H. FIELDER, GRAFTON STREET,

Which they secured at the unusually Large Discount of

57½ per cent off Cost Price.

The Stock comprises a Large Assortment of Mr. FIELDER'S own

TAILOR-MADE JACKETS, in the Latest Shades and Designs ;
ALSO A GREAT VARIETY OF

FRENCH AND GERMAN JACKETS, PLAIN,
TRIMMED WITH MINX, BEAVER,

SKUNK AND PERSIAN LAMB,

TRAVELLING CLOAKS AND RIDING JACKETS,
IN SHADES SUCH AS TABAC, CRIMSON, & DRAB BOX CLOTHS.

Fur Boas, Collaretts, Muffs, Trimmings, and Rugs, of
The Best Quality of Fur.

Our Own Large and Well-known Stock of JACKETS will be found Replete with the
Richest Novelties produced in

OTTO; NOGAT, ACCHEN, AGETHE, AND DRINDE JACKETS,
Trimmed with this Season's Fashion Fur.

RAIN AND TWEED TRAVELLING CLOAKS, CAPES, RICH SILK,
PLUSH AND FANCY CLOTHS.

Every Description of Fur at Half Price.

DRESS MATERIALS.
56-inch LADIES' SUITING TWEEDS, SERGES,
HABIT CLOTH, and CHEVIOT SERGES.
48-inch FRENCH VICUNA CLOTHS, CAMEL
HAIR CLOTHS, NEW PLAIDS, STRIPES, &c.

COSTUMES.
TAILOR-MADE FRENCH MODELS and TAILOR-MADE SKIRTS.

MANTLE BEAVER CLOTHS	in	Black, Blue, Fawn and Brown.
VICUNA CLOTHS	in	Black, Blue, and Grey
TWILLS	in	Black, Blue, Brown, and Fawn
BROCHE CLOTHS	in	Black and Fancy
MELTON CLOTHS	in	Black, Blue, Brown, and Fawn
BOX CLOTHS	in	Black, Blue, Brown, and Fawn

ASTRACHANS AND ROUGHS IN ALL SHADES.

We have arranged that during this Sale the other Departments, including the Carpets,
Cabinets, and Damasks, will offer their Goods at exceptionally Low Prices.

ARNOTT & CO., DUBLIN, LTD.

Advertisement from *The General Advertiser,* 26 November 1892

rival Henry Street Warehouse in the now vanished Denmark Street off the other side of Henry Street, but had a considerable reputation as a businessman. Kennedy, the shareholder who had prompted the unveiling of the assets, objected to this appointment but Molony was confirmed by 17 votes to 13.

At this meeting Elijah Hudson and Robert Bestick were also elected directors, bringing the total to seven; this cleared the way for the appointment of Henry Beater who, as company secretary, compiled invaluable records of the years between 1856 and 1933.

An advertisement of March 1883 shows the range and nature of Arnotts' trade in cloth and clothing and by 1886 important developments were reported in retail trading too. In that year two departments, woollens (suitings for men) and dresses (lighter materials for women), 'had been greatly enlarged by the addition of gentlemen's ready-made clothing and tailoring [made to measure], and ladies' and children's dressmaking; both branches are under the supervision of experienced cutters and all orders executed by our own work people on the premises'. The development of the sewing machine was opening the way for the major shift from clothes made by hand to clothes made by machine.

Development of the furniture trade was reported in March 1889 owing to the occupation and repair of numbers 9 and 10 Henry Street. The shallow fronts of these two houses were repaired for letting and the large space behind, running back beyond Prince's Street, was occupied by Arnotts' furniture, packing and dispatch departments. At the same time, the old facia which had been 'unsightly, cumbersome and dangerous' was removed from numbers 11 to 15 Henry Street and replaced; the wholesale entrance at number 15 had also been greatly improved.

The early death in 1891 of Elijah Hudson, who had proved himself a good wholesale manager, was a blow but annual reports under the chairmanship of Hamilton Reid read cheerfully, particularly that of February 1894 in which he said 'trading has been in advance of the previous year by a very considerable amount and we hope that the next time we meet, we may be able to give you perhaps a better account, another advance!'

By that date it had probably been forgotten that a directors' report of ten years earlier stressed that the stock at year end of £65,000 did not represent the average stock during the season, which might reach £90,000 or upwards, and that Robert Gardner had presciently declared in March 1887 that 'the suggested establishment of a reserve fund by a reduction of the dividend was a wise one; some exceptional loss might occur by fire or otherwise for which it would be desirable to have a reserve fund to draw upon'.

The stock destroyed in the great fire of 24 May 1894 was underinsured by £20,000.

3 DESTRUCTION AND RECONSTRUCTION 1894–1895

THE IRISH NEWSPAPERS devoted many columns, even whole pages, to lurid descriptions of the blaze which completely destroyed Arnotts' store and stock during the early morning of 4 May 1894. Here are some extracts from the *Dublin Evening Mail* of 4 May.

DESTRUCTIVE FIRE
BURNING OF ARNOTTS

Immense Destruction of Property

This morning, about twenty minutes past one o'clock, a fire which eventually proved of an unusually disastrous character, broke out in Messrs Arnotts and Co's large drapery and millinery emporium, 11 to 15 Henry Street. It originated, by some up to the present unexplained cause, in the large carpet store of the establishment, which extends as far back as Prince's Street. To summon the Fire Brigade and alarm the large staff of employees – who occupied rooms in the upper portion of the house fronting on Henry Street – seems to have been work of very little delay, for so far as can up to the present be ascertained, not one of the lives of the occupants appears to have been sacrificed to the terrible fury of the devouring element. The greater part of the staff of the firm, to the number of about a couple of hundred males and females, on becoming aware of the fire, with uncheckable rapidity rushed frantically to the balcony overhanging the street, in which a

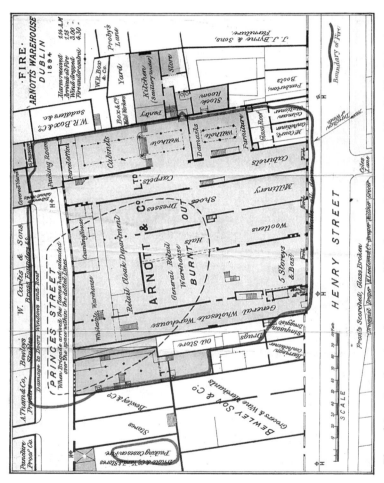

Plan of Arnotts, showing the extent of fire damage in 1894, issued by the Fire Brigade.

considerable crowd had already collected. By this time the flames had burst forth into the Henry Street frontage, and the distracted people, unfortunately, were at the side of the balcony furthest away from the counting house on the ground floor, where the ordinary access to the street is situated. The alarm prevailing at the time was indescribable, and what might have been the fate of a great number of the employees would have been terrible to anticipate but for the timely assistance which was forthcoming.

A police constable and three or four persons, with great promptitude and courage, breaking in one of the shutters, entered, and, risking the danger from smoke and flame, which was rapidly manifesting itself on all sides, made their way to the terror-stricken persons on the balcony.

Escape of the Inmates
The unfortunate occupants, many of whom were shrieking and gesticulating wildly with fear, were speedily assisted, or encouraged, to quit the premises in safety. A large number were carried through the accumulations of flames and smoke, while others, guided by the cool-headed venturers from outside, made their way with more or less difficulty to the street. In the mean time the Fire Brigade arrived on the scene, under Captain Purcell, and very soon every hydrant in the street, at the front, rear and sides, was sending its supply of water upon the building by rapidly adjusted hose. Hospitable assistance was all the time being proffered to the unfortunate creatures so summarily evicted from their sleeping rooms. Many were unable to snatch away with them any clothing to supplement their night garments, while a few others were more fortunate, perhaps because more cool-headed, and had succeeded in carrying away with them one or two portable articles or small handbags and portmanteaus.

The Brigade realised very soon after arrival that
the building was doomed to destruction. In the
heart of the building the flames spread with
tremendous fury, and at the rear the conflagration
assumed the most violent form. Enormous flames
shot up into the sky, which presented a lurid
appearance, while myriads of sparks flew upwards
and sprinkled the heavens as if sent forth by a
gigantic firework. The flames took a south-easterly
direction, and the Brigade despaired of saving any
portion of the establishment, which was in the
interior a gigantic mass of flame, through which
sections of the roof were falling in rapid succession
with terrible thuds. Every moment a fresh
clattering noise of falling slate, and portions of the
interior fitting told how rapidly the large building
was collapsing into a mere shell, composed of the
side and party walls. The Brigade had now turned
their attention to the safety of the adjoining
building at front and rear. Endeavouring to prevent
the fire from extending to the other side of Prince's
Street, the firemen worked indefatigably upon the
rear wall, which soon tumbled down with a terrific
crash. . . .

The frontage wall of Messrs Arnotts, in Henry
Street, remained intact for a long time after the
greater part of the interior was destroyed. The
patent shutters on the ground floor were the first to
give away, and, gradually, as if portion of a
transformation scene, the shutters were forced
asunder, and apertures presented little peep holes
through which the glare of the havoc inside
appeared like snatches of a brilliant spectacle
shortly to be fully unfolded. As soon as the full
brilliancy of the inside fury was clearly presented
the shutters began to fall away consumed like
matchwood, and the flames were presented with
striking vividness. It was soon after this period that
the upper portion of the front wall began to
collapse, thus allowing the unobstructed exposure

of the gigantic devastation of the flame in all its impressiveness. Smoke and flame shot out of the windows, dazzling and stifling alternately the firemen and the enormous crowd of anxious onlookers. The police, alive to the danger of allowing the public to stand within reach of the almost tottering walls, kept them well out of range of any sudden collapse. Volumes of smoke had just proceeded from the range of about half the frontage – the portion nearer to Sackville Street – when a startling development occurred. A fearful crash, appallingly deafening, rent the air, carrying with it a terrifying effect on the crowd gathered round.

Simultaneously with this terrible report the greater portion of the range of wall referred to – half the length of Messrs Arnotts' premises – collapsed with frightful suddenness, and everyone thought that at last destruction of human life had occurred in their midst.

Narrow Escape of Firemen
Three or four firemen were playing the hose at the time, and the instant impression was that they were buried beneath the overwhelming mass of debris. The horror experienced on all sides was not set at rest for a few moments, but it transpired that the men believed to have been stricken down had had a miraculous escape, although their lucky movements were unobserved amidst the vast cloud of dust and smoke spread around by the falling brickwork. The occurrence was an explosion of heated gas, generated on the premises, a common incident at large fires like this.

In response to a message from Captain Purcell, the Lord Mayor arrived upon the scene and, at the request of the Captain, his lordship communicated with the military authorities with a view to having the assistance of the soldiers to supplement the operations of the firemen. Before three o'clock about five hundred soldiers, including the whole of the Staffordshire Regiment and small detachments from other corps, put in an appearance from Ship Street Barracks. The military most ably seconded the efforts of the firemen not only in the manipulation of the hose but also as custodians of the public safety in keeping the crowd out of harm's way. Inspector Toole, who was in charge of the police, brought upon the scene as many constables as were available for the duty, and it must be said that their duties were discharged most energetically and effectively. A view of the vast conflagration from one of the upper windows of an adjoining house brought before the gaze perhaps the most comprehensive idea of the havoc wrought below. Walls and partitions mingled with flooring and ceilings in their headlong collapses, and sank into the depths of flames with an immense crash, causing blinding upheavals of smoke, sparks and flame. The glare of the sky overhead cast over the operations of all concerned in controlling the flames produced almost the effect of a powerful search light – reaching afar into the Heavens. With the approach of the grey dawn the disappearing darkness of the clouds was at times almost compensated for by the black wreaths of smoke issuing from the high burnt-out pile, and the flames, although gradually dying away, came into bolder prominence.

The male assistants in the establishment were evidently too excited and interested to seek the rest, which was freely offered to them, for they promenaded about the street in their state of semi-toilet during the entire morning. The successive collapses sounded like so many brisk cannonades until at a quarter past four o'clock one of the loudest sounds re-echoed around the adjoining thoroughfares. It sounded the fall of the last important remnant of the building, the remaining portion of the frontage in Henry Street. As the morning advanced the blazing and smouldering foundations were all that were left of Messrs Arnott's fine premises – literally burned to the ground.

Here is another extract from the *Dublin Evening Mail*, Saturday, 5 May 1894.

THE FIRE AT MESSRS ARNOTTS
THE BOOKS RECOVERED

Traffic Resumed in Henry Street

The books of Messrs Arnott and Company (Limited) were recovered last night. They were somewhat damp owing to the leakage of water from the rubbish lying on the ground into the strong room beneath where the books were stored. To clear away the pile of smouldering matter under which the apartment was buried was a work of great difficulty, and of some danger, as all portions of the debris were intensely heated, and in several places, when the surface matter was removed, flames burst suddenly forth. Three safes which lay outside the strong room were also recovered. Two of them seem to have suffered no damage. The third safe, which is a small one, was badly injured, but its contents have been found to be practically intact.

Clearing Henry Street
Astonishing progress has been made in the course of a few hours in the work of clearing the masonry which occupied the entire width of the thoroughfare in Henry Street for a distance of about 250 feet. A large number of men were set to work early this morning with pick and shovel to clear the rubbish from the street by piling it into a rampart extending along the pathway which bounds the space so lately occupied by the great warehouse. There are few people who on Friday evening could have been so sanguine as to expect traffic to be

resumed in Henry Street before noon on the
following day. But in this instance, as in many
others, it is the unexpected that has happened. So
successful were the workers in their efforts that
shortly after eleven o'clock the roadway was
almost completely cleared and vehicular traffic was
resumed. . . .

Messrs Arnott's Directors
The Director of Messrs Arnott and Company met
again at an early hour this morning in the Gresham
Hotel, and had under anxious consideration the
project of restarting business in temporary
premises as soon as possible. They had, however,
nothing new to communicate to the public, but
they seemed quite confident of being able in the
course of a very short time to make all preliminary
arrangements necessary for the speedy carrying out
of their laudable project. One of the proposals
before the meeting was to erect temporary premises
on the site of the old establishment, carrying on the
retail business in Henry Street and locating the
wholesale department in Prince's Street. The
inconvenience which would arise from this course
is obvious. An alternative suggestion was to
temporarily acquire premises suitable for the
business which might happen to be vacant. The
difficulty of finding at short notice premises
sufficiently extensive, and at the same time
centrally situated, is one of such great magnitude
that it is quite possible that the former course may
have to be pursued. With reference to the assistants,
it has been decided to send the young boys and the
ladies to their homes in the country.

The elder hands can remain in the city, or return
home at their discretion. In consequence of an
advertisement inserted by the directors in the
newspapers, the office of Mr. Beater, in Lower
Sackville Street, which has for the present been
placed at the disposal of the company, was

thronged at intervals throughout the day by
batches of assistants, who were paid their salaries
up to date. The gentlemen in charge of the office
were inundated with claims for goods, the property
of the customers, which had been entrusted to the
firm for repair. All claims that were found correct
were promptly paid. But the settlement of many
others had to be postponed pending an
examination of the books. In the repairing shops,
which were saved from burning simply because
they did not form part of the main building, there
are a large number of articles of furniture belonging
to the public, which are uninjured.

The drawing produced by the Fire Brigade (see page 28)
is of the site occupied by Arnotts in 1894; the dotted lines
show the extent of the blaze when the firemen arrived at
1.18 a.m. – four minutes after receiving the alarm! The
flames devouring the large amount of dry wood in the old
buildings were fanned by wind, which dropped at 3 a.m.;
by 4.30 a.m. the fire was stated to be under control. The
thick black line of the boundary of the fire shows that
everything on Arnotts' site was affected, and also the
shops on either side in Henry Street occupied by tenants of
Arnotts.

That was the early morning of Friday 4 May. That day
Sir John Arnott hurried by train from Cork to be met by his
grandson, Lauriston Arnott, who brought him to view the
smouldering ruins. To quote a letter written in 1943 by Sir
Lauriston, 'Old Sir John at once instructed them to go
ahead erecting windows etc., before waiting until the
bricks were cool.' This showed fine spirit and the correct
reaction of the trader – the impulse to restore the front
presented to the public at the earliest possible moment – as
a woman might repair her make-up.

The managers and directors had not been idle. By
Tuesday 8 May the *Dublin Evening Mail* reported that an
attempt had been made to secure the premises of Todd
Burns in Mary Street; this failed because Arnotts refused to
take the stock. There is no mention of this in minutes of

Arnotts' meetings; it was a natural idea for men in a hurry, but impractical. On Wednesday 9 May an advertisement on the back page of the *Evening Mail* announced in simple large type that the Round Room of the Rotunda was being fitted up for retail trading, that the directors had decided to erect an 'immense temporary building' on Arnotts' site which would give employment to staff and was expected to be ready in two to three weeks, and lastly that by arrangement with Fitzgerald, Cantwell & Co., Wine Merchants of 91, 92, 93 Abbey Street, space had been provided in the front part of their buildings where Arnotts' wholesale trade was being set up and customers would be met in a few days.

Not bad going! Even at this distance it may seem unfeeling to comment that the most striking thing about that advertisement of 9 May 1894 was its urgent 'modern' tone. It was Arnotts' first really good advertisement, produced in what we may be forgiven for calling the heat of the moment.

On Saturday 12 May the directors met, with Sir John Arnott in the chair. Present also were Hamilton Reid, Orlando Beater, Robert Bestick, O. P. Beater LLB and Henry Beater, secretary. Only Samuel Smalldridge was absent and he joined the other directors for a meeting on Tuesday 15 May and almost daily until the second week in June.

On Tuesday 15 May the superintendent on duty on the evening of 3 May attended the directors' meeting to report that on that evening he had visited every part of the premises after all employees had left and everything was in order. When he first saw the fire he believed it had originated at the rear of Mr Simpson's establishment – strictly speaking this meant somewhere along the site of number 16 Henry Street, probably in the back section occupied by Arnotts' goods entrance or 'wholesale warehouse' on the fire plan. As usual with fires in Arnotts the cause was not discovered; of many subsequent small fires the cause of only one can certainly be identified. It was started by the burning out of an unattended kettle used in a remote stock room for unauthorised tea making.

Cigarette butts carelessly thrown away by customers may have caused two others, but what is certain is that untidy accumulations of goods, old fixtures or other rubbish usually provided the fuel for these fires.

The meetings of directors from this date to the end of June 1894 are full of the sort of detail one would expect when re-establishing a trading business in a hurry, and naturally in a rough and ready way. Fifty large tables were bought from Brooks Thomas for £182 10s and fifty small tables for £125. Cummins, electrical contractors of Marlborough Street, whose descendant William Cummins joined Arnotts' staff in 1929, were paid £67 11s 8d for putting up 80 x 16 candle-power incandescent lights in the temporary shop on the old site, the work to be completed in fourteen days under a £10 penalty. Mr Simpson, tenant in number 16, was willing to surrender his lease which was to expire in four years; he accepted £400 for his rights and handed over his insurance claim of £750. £1,000 was accepted in full discharge of all claims for damage by fire to numbers 9 and 10 Henry Street. Mr Telford of Craig Gardner explained his method of finding out how far the stock was not covered by insurance. On 7 June Arnotts' £5 ordinary shares were quoted at £4 18s 9d.

A Lamson cash ball railway system was ordered for the temporary shop. (A set was still in operation in 1960 in Boyers of North Earl Street.)

The fire was a disaster that was felt most personally by the staff of Arnotts. A letter to *The Irish Times* from William Fry first called public attention to their plight, and William Fry & Son gave £25 towards the setting up of a fund. A letter from 'An Assistant' followed, calling attention to this fund, which had been set up by the Drapers' Club. In this letter the number of staff sleeping on the premises on the night of the fire was given as 120 men, 13 ladies and 14 apprentices; 72 further staff slept outside. Arnotts had sent the apprentices home, their fares paid. For the others, provision was made by a personal subscription of the directors themselves of £600, to which was added the insurance of £500 paid by Arnotts on behalf of the employed. This letter also mentioned 'outside hands such as seamstresses and other workers – a good many – who felt the disaster severely'.

The Lord Mayor of Dublin, Valentine Blake Dillon, then wrote in support of the fund quoting 'the saddest stories of young ladies and young men who had their entire savings in their trunks, with other little treasures that money would not purchase, all totally destroyed'. He also drew attention to 'ladies engaged in dressmaking in the house immediately adjoining Arnotts, to whom outside aid should be extended'.

Apart from the money subscribed by the directors and the insurance money, the only person named in directors' minutes was a Miss Cosgrave who was granted £5. However, on 1 June Robert Wallace 'attended with regard to re-engaging the retail hands' and on 5 June a Professor Bell offered to lodge twelve apprentices at 46 North Great George's Street for £2 a week. This meant the temporary premises was opening.

One of the earliest decisions on 12 May had been to appoint a Mrs Stritch as housekeeper. Her pay was raised on 28 June suggesting that she was by that time catering for staff meals. Before the fire, as the letter above confirmed, many staff and the apprentices were lodged as well as fed in Arnotts; after the fire only food was supplied; they were lodged elsewhere. In 1902, Alexander Nesbitt reported a letter from 'the hands' complaining about the food supplied: poor Mrs Stritch's catering was in question! She retired in 1919.

On Thursday 21 June Sir John chaired his last meeting. His signature of the minutes was extremely shaky. At that meeting the important decision to appoint George P. Beater as architect for the re-building at a fee of 2½ per cent was taken, despite the strong objections of Hamilton Reid who thought a public competition should be held.

From this date until his death in 1898 Sir John restricted himself to sending 'sundry letters' of good advice to which the company secretary was instructed to reply and which were if possible ignored – who is ever grateful for gratuitous advice? Here is the text of one dictated on 17 March 1896 and sent to Orlando Beater. Sir John is clearly being sent detailed information about the progress of the departments. Note also his livelier ideas of stock-turn.

> You should tell your Clerk to mark on the weekly sheet how many times each of the buyers have been to the markets since the beginning of the Half Year and continue to do so during the rest of the term as it is of the greatest importance to have fresh goods and in many cases they need not buy over a couple of hundred pounds.
>
> Some of your departments are in a deplorable state notably the Bonnets, the turn over seems to be about twice a year but should be six times at least. Look at the Shirts, Child's Dresses and many others.

The business was restored remarkably quickly after the disaster of the fire. Sales for the week ending 28 July 1894 were £2,225 retail and £2,300 wholesale. That was probably two-thirds of the normal level. The temporary shop on site in Henry Street was in full swing and the Rotunda was no longer required; there are no details of the trade there. In August the assessor, Walter Hume of 50 Dame Street, was being asked for a prompt payment of the £29,000 agreed as the value of the destroyed buildings. The total claim, including stock and fixtures, was £45,063.

On 22 November the architect, George Beater, after visits 'to London and other cities' put plans before the directors. He had already been asked to show them to Sir John for his opinion. A week later he was instructed to build in Prince's Street from the wall of number 16 for about eighty feet 'towards the temporary building' to a width of thirty feet for the wholesale – this area corresponds with that marked 'wholesale warehouse' on the fire plan.

This suggests that the 'temporary shop', (see the photograph on page 40) for which there is no plan, ran from Henry Street back to Prince's Street. From its photograph it appears to have had a frontage on Henry Street of about thirty feet widening to more than double width behind the space occupied by the letting of numbers 9 and 10 Henry Street. On the fire plan this might have been the area

Work on the temporary store, on the burnt-out site, began immediately; this is what it looked like in May 1894

The facade of the temporary store on the old site, June 1894

occupied before the fire by half the millinery, shoes and dresses and all of the cabinets, carpets and damasks. It was quite natural that managers would copy what existed even in temporary premises. In fact, the rebuilt store was designed as a bigger and better edition of what had been destroyed (see architect's sketch on title page).

On 4 December it was decided to seek estimates from the following builders: Good, Pile, Collen Brothers and H. & J. Martin; that of H. & J. Martin was accepted.

The beginning of 1895 was occupied with the financial reconstruction of the company of which, it was recorded on 22 February, Sir John Arnott was now in favour. Sir John was represented at meetings of this time by John George Moore. Mr Clay of Casey, Clay & Collins, with counsel's opinion, provided the necessary legal advice.

A circular letter to shareholders dated 16 March 1895 informed them that the net profit for the year to 31 January had been maintained, but that counsel's opinion was that because no dividend could be paid until the loss occasioned by the fire had been extinguished (good word in the circumstances!) a scheme for re-construction of the company was annexed with formal notice of an extra-ordinary general meeting at the Gresham Hotel.

Due to the ill-health of Hamilton Reid, the chair at this meeting was taken by Orlando Beater, who proposed at unusual length the scheme of reconstruction, which was further explained by Clay. Telford of Craig Gardner and Smalldridge, supporting the motion, were the only other speakers. The proposal was welcomed by the shareholders and the newspapers. The share price had fallen and at least one report – in the *Irish Investors' Guardian* of August 1894 – had greatly exaggerated the losses. This was surprising since the same *Investors' Guardian* of June 1894 had chosen a figure, from among those circulating, which proved remarkably accurate at £30,000.

The reconstruction balance sheet shows the total fire loss at £30,528. With premises and goodwill at the 1894 figures – some outlay on temporary building, furnishing and dividends for the year 1894 balanced by net profit of £15,277 – there remained £30,040 to write down out of capital. This was done by reissuing the £60,000 of debentures at 4 per cent, but replacing the former £150,040 worth of £5 ordinary shares by 15,000 £5 6 per cent cumulative preference shares £4 paid-up and 15,000 £5 ordinary shares £4 paid-up – thus the paid-up share capital was reduced to £120,000. So, to the evident relief of shareholders, the company was 'reconstructed'.

The immediate cost was that shareholders' dividends totalled on preference and ordinary shares only £8,400 instead of £12,129 of previous years, and a fifth of their equity was converted into a call on the new shares, of which again half had been changed into preference shares. But the trade and the goodwill had been preserved.

Interior of the new store, looking towards the main entrance along the central aisle, late 1890s, photographed from the stairs leading up to the first floor back. This picture could almost have been taken in the 1930s.

4 REBUILDING AND RECOVERY 1895–1910

THE FIRE HAD shocked everyone in Arnotts. All desired to return as quickly as possible to normal. The directors and managers were united in determination to rebuild the business and conserve in future its hard-earned resources. They and the staff achieved a miracle in that the trade was only briefly interrupted and Arnotts was quickly rebuilt.

It was indeed rebuilding; this time to a design resembling the old Arnotts which had been cobbled together from the various houses acquired on Henry Street. The new building was of a relatively large size for its period in Dublin; when wholesale was taken out of the lower ground floor into Abbey Street in the 1950s an amazing extent of wooden floor was found. It had been laid in 1898 for stretching, tacking and cutting carpets but in the 1950s not much more than half was in use. The whole undertaking was clearly ambitious.

As for conservation of resources the directors, older as well as younger, and the younger managers coming up to board level, all showed their determination to hold the dividend on the ordinary shares at about half the net profits, instead of paying away the greater part. The rate of 8 per cent continued until the £1 call on the preference and ordinary shares was wiped out in 1913; after that, with the growing profits of wartime, dividends also began to increase.

Of the remaining older men, Sir John Arnott was to die in 1898, and Hamilton Reid retired in 1895; the latter took the chair at directors' meetings until his retirement but had relied on Orlando Beater to preside at the extraordinary general meeting in the Gresham Hotel in March 1895. John

Hamilton Reid had obviously been deeply shocked by the fire but rubicund Orlando Beater struggled on until his retirement at the age of eighty-three in 1903, yielding the chair at annual general meetings in 1900 and 1901 to Samuel Smalldridge. John Hamilton Reid was replaced as non-executive director by James Carlyle.

The rebuilding was done in three main sections. As we have seen, the wholesale area along Prince's Street came first. Presumably this was because the temporary building on the western side of the site, that is, nearest to Liffey Street, was considered satisfactory enough for the retail trade, not because wholesale was regarded as more important. The front on Henry Street was then put in place. In March 1898, at the annual general meeting, Orlando Beater announced that trading was moving into the second section built; but he confessed he was then 'pretty old and he should say he had never gone through as much as he had during the last four years'.

The rebuilding did drag on, not helped by a strike of building workers of four months' duration. This caused unfavourable comment in the *Irish Investors' Guardian* on 5 March 1898 in a report which was otherwise encouraging. In March 1899 the completion of the Henry Street front allowed the shareholders to meet in what was for years to be called the boardroom. The contractors had promised completion in three months of the rest of the western side giving additional space for the furniture, carpet and curtain trade. By that time the basement was lighted by electricity. The lifts and the Lamson pneumatic cash system worked off the same engines. The directors looked forward to ridding the site of the inconvenient temporary building.

The *Irish Investors' Guardian* – what a reassuring title! – gave lists of shareholders in Arnotts at the time, apologising for not including those with less than forty shares (£4 paid) because they were 'exceedingly numerous'.

At the annual general meeting of March 1897 Orlando Beater remarked that two-thirds of the shareholders were ladies, and this feminine profile seems to have persisted. Arnotts' chairmen frequently appealed to the ladies to patronise the store – or rather the 'warehouse' as it was often called around the end of the century – but the absence of women shareholders from annual general meetings was noted and regretted.

In 1896 and 1897 the euphoria of the recovery of trade immediately after the fire had evaporated and profits were more difficult to find. Profits in these two years for Pim Brothers, which had been running most years at over £18,000 – about £2,000 above Arnotts – also dropped. At Arnotts' weekly board meetings failures of wholesale customers were more frequently mentioned; there were no less than four on 13 January 1898 when it was reported to the directors that sundry wholesale accounts were slow, large and without security.

The wholesale manager at the time, the bright-eyed, bearded Robert Wallace, was evidently considered to be doing his best; he was co-opted a director with a salary of £350 in April 1898. The retail manager was Alexander Nesbitt, who reported to the directors in March of the same year that he had interviewed a Mr Freeland for the position of buyer of the readymade department, and had been authorised to engage him at £120 a year; buyers could qualify for bonuses to stretch this rather small salary. (At this time an unskilled labourer could earn about £50 a year; middle-class respectability required as much as £250 a year.) Freeland was still buyer until the Second World War and his daughter Susan spent her working life in the central management office.

Difficult trading conditions obviously turned directors' attention from the excitement of ordering buildings and equipment to the less glamorous task of finding money to pay for them. Hence the increased financial detail in the minutes. Accounts for expenditure were queried and at times challenged, including in the end the final accounts for the building. Bad debts in the first half of 1898 amounted to £272 in retail trade and £807 in wholesale; retail trade had then and always the enormous advantage of being more for cash than for credit, a tendency that had become much more marked forty-five years later.

A surprising feature of Arnotts' financing emerged in the minutes of this time. Deposits by about forty customers

The new store ready for customers early in the century: (above) ladies' cloaks (below) furniture and bedding

totalled some £71,000 whereas bank borrowing was only one-tenth of that. Since interest rates were falling decisively, and Arnotts had not reduced the deposit rate, the company secretary was forced to ask the directors in January 1899 whether any limits should be placed on the increasing deposit accounts. The following July a limit of £1,000 was applied.

From 1876 deposits had been included in Arnotts' balance sheets in 'sundry trade and cash creditors'. Since this item was always larger than stock in trade, instead of smaller, there was room in it to conceal these very considerable deposits on which, in early 1899, interest at the rate of 4 per cent was being paid.

The two general managers or the company secretary brought to directors' meetings not only the engagement and discipline of managers, but also unusual matters such as advertising and even merchandising. They reported appointments such as that of Owen Clancy, the buyer of the hosiery department – Alexander Nesbitt's old department – at £130 a year, and Mr Sweeney to buyer of the glove department at £100 a year. Even with bonuses these modest salaries seem to compare badly with that of the retail department manager of Easons round the corner in Sackville Street who earned over £200 a year. An unusual appointment was that of Dr Moran as medical officer of the company; his salary was increased to £180 for the extra work caused by the lodging out of staff after the fire.

An important decision of the directors in November 1898 was to remove the price limit on costumes sold in the mantle department. This was presumably inspired by Alexander Nesbitt's often stated intention to trade up in Arnotts retail. The following part of Samuel Smalldridge's address to the shareholders in March 1900 spelt out the policy.

> We have recently been making a great feature of Ladies 'high class' dressmaking, and with such success that Arnott's Mantles, Dresses, Tailormade Costumes, and Millinery are the talk and admiration not only of Dublin, but of Cork, Galway

Directors of Arnotts (from a photomontage of 1907)

Samuel Smalldridge

James Carlyle

Robert Wallace

Alexander Nesbitt

Robert Bestick

O. P. Beater

and other large cities. In the section of the premises
just handed over to us by the builders, special
accommodation has been provided for this
important branch of our business and I invite lady
shareholders – I am sorry there are not some of
them present – and customers to inspect those
rooms. They will see how nicely they are equipped
and how comfortably the workers are provided for;
we shall have no cause to dread the visits of the
factory inspector, for they will find every point of
sanitation has been amply meet. We are glad to say
that the final portion of the building – which is only
a corner at the back – is now in the hands of the
Contractors, who, we hope, will complete the work
during the Summer.

You will then be the Proprietors of a really
magnificent block of buildings and one of the very
best drapery warehouses in the Kingdom.

Presiding at annual general meetings in place of old
Orlando Beater, Smalldridge is worth quoting again in
March 1902 for he spoke more plainly than was usual then.

You will notice that what we mentioned last year is
now an accomplished fact, that is the consolidation
of our three classes of debentures, bearing different
rates of interest into one debenture stock bearing 4
per cent. Your Directors are greatly pleased with
this achievement, and the easy way it was
accomplished, and we think that the shareholder
also will be glad, as it shows what is thought of
their property in the City of Dublin.

He went on to say that the previous year's record results
had been slightly exceeded and that £3,000 had been added
to the reserve fund. 'There is nothing sensational about our
business,' he concluded, 'only plain hard work day by day
and it takes plenty of that to make £18,000 a year.'

This clear statement of financial and trading policy was
also to be furthered by somewhat timid ventures into
advertising. It was decided in April 1898 not to pay £5 for

one month's display of advertisements 'upon a screen to be exhibited by the Bazaar at the Rotunda in view of Sackville Street'. But in the autumn of that year Easons' proposed contract for advertising for a year in twenty-five selected railway stations at £50 was accepted. In November space was booked in the Christmas number of *The Irish Times*, and by October 1901 Arnotts had worked up to discussing advertising schemes with *The Irish Times* and agreed to a three-year contract for three front page insertions a week at 24s 9d.

Unusual subjects at directors' meetings included a request from Alexander Nesbitt that stocktaking should not be undertaken during the month of July because of the inconvenience and loss of trade occasioned. Half-yearly stocktakings were abolished again during the 1960s and 1970s because it was realised that buyers, except for the most successful and courageous, 'squeezed' their stocks. This produced an acceptably low total for the date of the stocktaking but lost sales because the goods in most demand had been sold and were not replaced until stock-taking was over.

Other subjects included the resignation of Cummins & Sons from the superintendence of the engine room at the end of July 1899; they were agents for the Crossley engine which produced the 70 volt electric light for the new building. Maguire & Gatchel's tender of £387 for low pressure hot water heating was accepted – to supplement J. Grandy's hot air plants! We believe that this low pressure water heating system, with repeated tinkering and alteration, was still in operation in 1947 when the most unusually cold February made conditions in Arnotts numbing beyond belief. The lack of good fuel was no help then, but the real failure was in design – there was simply no separate flow and return.

Failures there were in the new Arnotts building but other features were imaginative and successful. Alexander Nesbitt claimed credit for preventing the architect from including many more pillars (he referred to 'a forest of pillars') but the idea of using the central hollow pillars as drains for rainwater from the wide expanse of well-lighted flat central roof, was quite unusual for its time. The separation of the work into three may have caused additional pillars. In the end, the numerous pillars were used by director Patrick J. O'Connor, followed by his son Michael, to create, with a few more pillars and the reinforcement of their bases below ground level, a most valuable mezzanine floor over most of the area of the 1900 building; this work was undertaken in stages between 1950 and 1975.

With all the excitement of the 1890s it is not surprising that we now begin to hear more from the rank and file members of Arnotts staff.

The directors had worried about members of staff in old age or serious ill-health and created in Patrick Reid's time the benevolent fund, which was brought up to £1,500 in early 1902. They had also helped managers and buyers to buy endowment insurance by paying half the premiums. But now conditions of employment were beginning to be queried.

Our first examples are somewhat negative; in December 1900 Robert Wallace proposed that 'the young men's sitting room be allocated to travellers showing their goods to our buyers up to 11 a.m. each day and buyers to enter via the counting house and a boy to be kept to go for any buyer'. This room was evidently on the first floor level in Henry Street and could be reached by the stairs at the western end of the building, but the buyers were to run the gauntlet of the counting house to reach it. Bestick asked for time to consider the idea and, if it ever happened, it was at least at an hour when staff should be so busy in their departments as to prevent them sitting anywhere.

In March 1899 'the wholesale hands' asked for a half-holiday; it was refused 'until it became general'. Easons had introduced a half-holiday for staff in 1865!

But small reliefs for staff came about this time; Arnotts closed shop one Wednesday in June 1898 for an athletic sports meeting. The Royal visit to Dublin in April 1900, the death of Queen Victoria in 1901 and the Coronation of Edward VII each caused the whole store to be closed for

A photomontage of senior staff in 1907

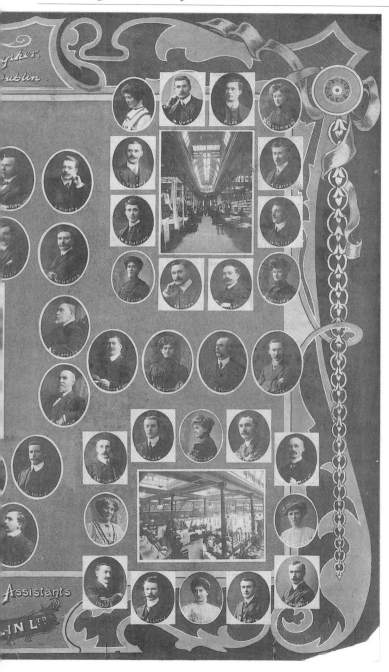

the day. It is hoped the staff were paid on all three occasions – only one of them is mentioned in minutes.

In June 1902 the Irish Drapers' Assistants' Association was mentioned for the first time in directors' minutes; it was refused closure for a half-day's sports. In December 1902 the Association reappeared asking for discussion of Christmas holidays. In 1904 came its formal request to the Merchant Drapers' Association and to Arnotts for early closing on one day a week (the weekly half-holiday). Some of the merchants must have been easier, but to both requests, and in particular to a Mr Farmer of Clery & Co., Arnotts gave dusty answers. It is not surprising therefore to learn that staff in Arnotts were prominent in early union organisation in the trade; the Assistants' Association started in 1901 with an address in 56 Henry Street. Its founder was Michael O'Lehane who was a native of Fermoy and was working in Arnotts' carpet department at the time. Two other members of Arnotts' staff attended the first minuted meeting of the drapery branch committee; there was a total attendance of seventeen.

In May 1902 the excellent Samuel Smalldridge died and Alexander Nesbitt, retail manager, was co-opted in his place. It is believed that Alexander's first thought was to ask the company secretary, Henry Beater, what would happen if there was disagreement between himself as retail managing director and Robert Wallace, the wholesale managing director. The unforgettable reply was 'The stronger mind will prevail'. Since both men received £100 bonuses in August 1902, the intention seems to have been to treat them as equals; Robert Wallace's salary in 1898 had been £350 on his co-option as director and both he and Alexander were brought up to £500 in February 1900. In April 1903 the two men interviewed William Armstrong of Switzers and engaged him as buyer of ribbons, flowers and parasols.

Robert Wallace was elected chairman of the directors on the resignation of Orlando Beater in 1903. From the earliest days of the public company, the chairman of Arnotts has been elected (and almost invariably re-elected) by his fellow directors immediately after each annual general meeting or on the retirement or death of his precursor. The new chairman must surely have sealed his popularity with a gift of £1,000 to the benevolent fund. Alexander Nesbitt is reported as saying at the general meeting of 1904 that he would testify to the depth and sincerity of the new chairman's interest in his fellow workers over many years. But neither believed in spoiling the staff.

Robert Wallace, who had started work thirteen years before Alexander Nesbitt, was a colourful character; the latter was comparatively reserved and quiet. There has never been any suggestion in Nesbitt mythology that relations between the two men were other than cordial; perhaps Alexander's caution helped.

As acting chairman at the 1903 general meeting Robert Wallace declared 'We propose to put every surplus shilling into reserves. It is our earnest desire to pass on to your successors a stable security.' This was certainly Alexander Nesbitt's intention too, so it is a little surprising to read in the minutes of 11 February 1905 that the usual dividend of 8 per cent was agreed only after considerable discussion. Orlando Beater having resigned, the remaining directors were Robert Bestick (elected 1887), who had started work in Arnotts about the same year as Alexander Nesbitt, with O. P. Beater from 1892 and James Carlyle from 1894 as the non-executive directors. The opposition was not allowed to check the steady rebuilding of Arnotts' finances, which it became necessary to treat as lightly as possible in front of the shareholders. In 1907 Robert Wallace spoke of 'our good old friend the 8 per cent'. Support for the policy came at that time from the *Irish Investors' Guardian* which, commenting on the success of public companies such as Pim Brothers and Arnotts, said of Arnotts: '£6,000 to reserve and £4,000 forward. Lucky shareholders. Thrift will tell.' Fortunately the shareholders seemed grateful enough.

The Beater family was still strongly represented at board level, but this may not always have been an advantage. The architect of the new building, George Beater, was in the end allowed only 2½ per cent commission on the main buildings and 5 per cent on all outside work – a total of £2,590. He was held to be largely responsible for the quarrel leading Arnotts into taking an unsuccessful action against the builder H. & J. Martin, and it was thought he ought to have contributed substantially more to the cost of this than the £500 he had offered. However, when Orlando Beater handed in a cheque for £500 on George Beater's behalf, the directors relented and paid George a balance of £250 and an honorarium of £500. After all, as Robert Wallace is recorded as saying, 'These fine premises have been erected at half the fee usually received by architects.'

In the minutes of a directors' meeting in March 1906 the architect (presumably George Beater) is recorded as attending about proposed alterations to numbers 9 and 10 Henry Street. Possession of these two shallow shops on Henry Street having been secured, J. & P. Good rebuilt them in time for Robert Wallace to declare to shareholders at the general meeting of March 1908:

> Doubtless you have noticed we are adding a new Lung to our Furnishing Departments, and that you may appreciate the pressing necessity for this increased breathing space I have only to mention (what will surprise you) that the centre of the building is wider by one-third than the frontage in Henry Street. The result is, for our twenty-five Drapery Departments we have only ten Show Windows, and the three important Furnishing Departments which contribute so largely to our turnover and earning power are completely hidden from the street. We carry large stocks in these Departments, and for anything the man or woman in Henry Street can see of the goods they might as well be in the Park. This unsatisfactory state of things will now be remedied. The forty feet of frontage we are adding will enable us to have two splendid Show Windows, with a handsome and special entrance to this important branch of our business.[1]

---

[1] This arcade disappeared in the 1959 rebuilding of numbers 7 to 10 Henry Street.

Table 4.1: Profits and dividends in Irish department stores 1906–7 and 1907–8

| | | 1906–7 | | 1907–8 | |
| | | Net Profits | Dividends | Net Profits | Dividends |
Store	Location	£	%	£	%
Arnotts	Dublin	19,742	8	19,865	8
Pims	Dublin	19,726	6	19,402	6
Lyons	Cork	14,060	6	17,301	6.5
Switzers	Dublin	12,302	10	12,140	10
Dwyers	Cork	10,493	8	10,643	8
Cannocks	Limerick	9,269	9	9,310	9
Crowe, Wilson	Dublin	7,370	8	7,562	8
Cash	Cork	7,008	7	7,431	7
M'Birney	Dublin	5,515	6	5,647	6
Henry St W'house	Dublin	4,431	11.25	4,909	11.25
Webbs	Dublin	2,670	6.25	3,005	6.25

Source: *Irish Investors' Guardian* 7 March 1908

Note: 1908 was the 25th consecutive year in which Arnotts had declared an 8% dividend.

Robert Wallace earned a reputation as an 'orator of commerce'. The *Irish Investors' Guardian* of March 1909 noted that 'Mr Wallace is a master of cheery metaphor'. Reporting on Arnotts' general meeting of March 1907, *The Leprechaun* (an early version of *Dublin Opinion*) referred to 'the picturesque unconventionality of the Chairman's address [which] had so enchanted the audience that, if the dividend had been nil instead of the substantial eight, they would have smiled and said, "The address was worth the money". Undoubtedly one of the most striking and brilliant contributions to the commercial oratory of our time.'

Sadly the colourful Robert Wallace died on 8 December 1909 in his late sixties.

As a final tribute to him we print words from a draft in his handwriting of what may have been a speech for the annual general meeting of 1910:

> May I not with perfect propriety thankfully express the grateful appreciation of those who, having been

for many years in the thick of the fight, having known and felt every pulsation of the business, and who have sought day by day to keep in step with the advanced, and to stimulate the lagging forces, as they steadily pushed their way inch by inch over well trodden commercial fields, keenly contested by strong but honourable opponents, and occasionally through ditches thickly lined with modern sharp shooters on to firm high ground; and on that high level had the privilege of lending a hand to our special earning power, firmly planting and yearly steadying our grand old standard the 8 per cent. I say again is it any wonder I should seek to voice the feelings of our united thankfulness.

Robert Wallace, sometime racey horseman, sometime sailor, and finally faithful military leader – rest in peace.

5 TOWARDS WAR AND TROUBLES 1910–1922

THE DEATH OF Robert Wallace left the field clear for his junior in management, Alexander Nesbitt, who was elected chairman in December 1909. William Wallace, wholesale manager, younger brother of Robert, was co-opted to return the number of directors to five, of whom three were either non-executive or retired.

Alexander Nesbitt, having shown determination on his appointment as director to have his way, had proved to be the reliable partner of his more lively senior. They agreed completely on policy, clearly intending to make the company very strong financially: certainly to remove any goodwill from the balance sheet, and also to write down the biggest asset of all – the premises.

Alexander was tall and reasonably handsome. He was down to earth, not given to frills, the son of a farmer of Randalstown, Co. Antrim. At the age of sixteen a friend bought him an apprenticeship in John Arnott & Co. of Dublin; Alexander had said he was tired of hoeing turnips on frosty mornings. His education can only have been rudimentary secondary; his assets were his determination to succeed, and his puritanical lack of self-indulgence. His only known deviation from work was to play a good game of billiards (he could on occasion make a break of a hundred); apart, that is, from fathering five sons, and two daughters who did not survive. Of course, his sons' upbringing and education – in three cases to the completion of professional degrees in Trinity College, Dublin – held him to the shop floor. He died in 1941, in his ninetieth year, bored with life and too fond of a glass of whiskey.

The facade of the new shop at the turn of the century

His beloved wife, Elizabeth, died before him in 1936. He had by then achieved a solid middle-class lifestyle, Turkey-carpeted, mahogany-dining-room-tabled, leather-chaired, but had long ago given up the only occupations of his retirement which were walking round Dalkey Hill and reading Shakespeare. Standing round that dining-room table at his Presbyterian funeral the eye of the author, his eldest grandson, fell on a table mat with what was surely his encouraging final message: 'Cheerio'!

Alexander had been promoted to retail manager, he said, because he had once proved to the satisfaction of the 'counting house' that he had a better grasp of the trading figures in his hosiery department than they had, and general managers were always thought to be hard to find. But in his first important management decision he made, or concurred in, the mistake of appointing Maurice Power to replace William Wallace as wholesale manager. Power was discovered shortly afterwards in his office with a girl on his knee. The poor man was dismissed.

Alexander's sons protested that this was harsh treatment but, since they were young men, at most in their mid- or early twenties, they were able to view the offence more lightly. Presumably the girl was on the staff and the occasion was considered destructive of management authority. Frank Hallinan succeeded Power in buying for the hosiery department; his son Clement started in Arnotts in the early 1940s and became a most successful wholesaler traveller in the Cork area.

In 1910 a keen introductory offer by the International Sprinkler Co. for protecting the whole building in Henry Street was accepted – fire was not to be allowed to destroy it a second time. In the same year, with the advice of an engineer, a Mr Tatlow of Trinity College, on the electric lighting system, a new dynamo and producer plant were ordered. Alexander also showed his feeling for trade by having a 'veranda' erected across the pavement in Henry Street at recently occupied numbers 9 and 10. This allowed the ladies to reach the arcade to the

Staff excursion to the Spa Hotel, Lucan, 10 July 1915

furnishing departments from their carriages without fear of rain, hail or snow.[1]

But the initial achievement of the new chairman is best read in the company accounts between 1910 and 1913. The net profit for the year 31 January 1910 exceeded £20,000 for the first time since the fire; it hardly varied in the three years following and after 1911 Alexander never stressed it. Instead, his businesslike address to shareholders pointed to sales, which in 1910 were the largest ever, and to expenses, which were the lowest on record. In that year, sundry creditors and cash on deposit fell sharply from £60,000 to £33,000 by the elimination of much of the remaining deposit taking: the rate of interest paid had been reduced from 4 to 2½ per cent. Stocks were about 9 per cent lower despite the increased sales, and debtors up by only 5 per cent due to increased wholesale trade. The most striking reduction was of £20,000 in premises and goodwill compared with the year before.

By 1913 creditors were down to £21,000, reserves up to a peak of £20,000, premises and goodwill down to £110,000 and stocks to £54,000. Cash in hand again stood at £13,000. (Arnotts' records make no reference to the long painful lockouts of 1913 in Dublin but, as already noted, wars and rebellion were not written up in Arnotts.)

The figures above represent the tucking away of profits, which were not soaked up by allowing other assets to rise. They were achieved by closer management of trading and of the sales staff. Commission was introduced on retail sales and the old system of premiums or 'spiffs' abolished. 'Spiffs' were small payments to concentrate sales effort on goods which were 'sticking', instead of clearing them at reductions in price. It was at this time that the foundations were laid of the continuing reputation of Arnotts' Sales, of which only two in the year are allowed, in July and January. And at last the staff were given a Saturday half-holiday, advertised to customers on 10 April 1912.

---

[1]The veranda was removed in the 1940s when Patrick O'Connor built a canopy from 11-15 Henry Street, later extended along the entire frontage of Arnotts.

Alexander deliberately chose Saturday: Wednesday was the more usual half-day north of the Liffey – only Todd Burns and Clerys on the north side followed Alexander's example. He wished Arnotts to be classed with the more up-market stores, particularly those on the south side of the Liffey such as Switzers and Pim Brothers.

He did not doubt his judgement in this, and indeed was always ready to back it, never waiting upon the decisions of fellow traders. It is not surprising that he gave a cool reception in July 1911 to letters proposing an employers' federation – the Merchant Drapers' Association. Nor did the directors of Arnotts at first welcome the establishment of the Distributive Workers' Union.

In his political outlook Alexander was naturally a Redmondite home-ruler, which must have been the usual stance at the time of non-conformists in business circles. Arnotts supported the development of new industries such as the splendid Provident Woollen Mills of Foxford, Co. Mayo and contributed money to the Dublin Exhibition of 1882; a larger part was played with ten windows of Irish-made goods at the time of the 1907 Exhibition. As we have seen, workrooms established in Arnotts for women's costumes and dresses and men's suits, and indeed for furniture-making and carpet and curtain fitting, were normal industrial activities of a department store at the time; the increased space in the new building of 1898 helped this trend.

We may think it is only in recent times that stock market analysts predict the future trend of company figures and newspaper business columns count chickens before they are hatched, but a pioneer of the movement can be read in the *Irish Investors' Guardian* report of Arnotts' annual general meeting of 1913. In concluding a thorough appraisal of the figures of the previous year to 31 January it expressed 'surprise that they do not place a higher value on their property. A few more years of good results and the continuance of the present methods of finance will almost compel an increased dividend.'

Alexander had removed the £1 call (£5 share, £4 paid-up) on the preference and ordinary shares a year before, and in the following year, 1914, he took the hint; a bonus of 2s 6d on the ordinary shares brought the total dividend in the year to 11⅛ per cent. £1,000 was distributed among the non-executive directors and, for the first time on record, the monthly staff got an extra month's pay and the rest an extra week. The chairman must have felt comfortable about the prospects, although he was surely conscious that war with Germany was not far off.

In 1915 Robert Bestick died. He had started in Arnotts in 1867, about the same time as Alexander, but was very much his senior. He had been retail manager before Alexander and a director since 1887. James Cooke J.P. was co-opted in his place. The chairman made few comments about the world outside Arnotts in his addresses to annual general meetings but in March 1916, he praised James Cunningham,[2] for his efforts as retail manager in keeping the business going when supplies were so difficult to obtain. He also declared, rather prophetically, 'It is a matter for profound thankfulness that we have been able to carry on the business of the company in peace during the troubled times through which we are passing, while the world around us is engaged in war. Perhaps in days to come we may be called upon to pass through difficulties of a more trying and perplexing nature.'

Certainly the destruction in central Dublin during the Rising in Easter Week 1916 came very close to the store in Henry Street. The chairman's annual report, as covered in the *Evening Mail* of 3 March 1917, referred to

> . . . an eventful period in the history of the company. When they looked around they saw on almost all sides the desolation that prevailed, yet they were permitted to meet in that room in peace and quietness as if nothing had happened. A couple of thousand pounds would cover the injury to their property. The escape that they had had was

---

[2]He had been appointed buyer of the costume department in November 1911, at a salary of £450 a year, on the resignation of a Miss McCormack.

almost miraculous. Fire had broken out in two places, they had three shells as souvenirs, and the tower was perforated by bullets and shrapnel. One shell had struck a water-pipe and water flowed for two days and nights damaging £10-£12,000 worth of goods. However, they sold off these goods very cheaply, which proved a cheap advertisement.

Two other documents survive of the rebellion as seen from inside Arnotts. The first is a daily report by the super-intendents on duty from Tuesday 25 April, the day after Easter Monday when it began, to the following Monday 1 May.

Tuesday 25/4/16

Day duty. Swords. Ryan. Cowman.
Night duty. Swords. Ryan.
Looting went on all day.
Williams. Henry Street. Looted and set on fire.
About 6 men taken to hospital. Shot in Henry Street.
During the night three large windows broken.
Ryan and Cowman visited the 'O' Division re help if
*   necessary.*

Wednesday 26th

Day duty. Swords. Ryan and Cowman.
Night duty. Ryan and Cowman.
Monaghan and Farrell secured doors and windows.
Looting went on all day and most of the night in Henry
*   Street.*
About 9 people shot. Passed up to Jervis Street.
During the night we got great assistance from Messrs
*   O'Brien, Marks, Green and O'Connor in keeping the*
*   looters in check.*

Thursday 27/4/16

Day duty. Ryan and Cowman.
Night duty. Ryan and Cowman.
Looting in the morning up to 12 o'clock.

Streets very dangerous.

Bullet broke a lot of glass in front of Warehouse.[3]

*Volunteers broke in through Princess [sic] St, parcel
office door commandeered about 500 worth of goods.
Paid 5 visits during the day, carried the goods away in
mail sacks. (Mr. Cunningham has list of depts and
probable amounts).*

*Three Volunteers entered the Warehouse through
Princess St. door and took possession of the tower.
Inspected the tailors' workrooms, used our ladders and
barricaded themselves with pieces of dress goods in the
tower.*

*Six Volunteers got on the Warehouse roof, broke in
through Trimmings Department, smashed the locks of
Mangan's door and W.S. Garage door. Seeking means
of retreat if necessary through the house. We gave
them a ladder.*

Clerys shelled and burned during the night.

Friday 28/4/16

Streets very dangerous. Volunteers leave tower.

Volunteers ask for the making of a flag.

We left the Warehouse crossed over to Webbs opposite.

Warehouse shelled about 12 o'clock.

Portion of sprinkler broken off, representing three heads.

*Water running from 12 o'clock until Corporation
Official entered the house on Sunday.*

*Military arrived about 5.30 stopped fire alarm bell with
rifle shots and escorted us behind barrier in Britain
Street.*

Post Office set on fire.

*Remained with Mrs Fanning, Rathdown Tce, from
Friday night until Monday morning.*

---

[3] 'Warehouse' was evidently the name used by staff to describe the department store.

Monday 1st May 1916

Returned to Warehouse and had urgent repairs made.
Monahan and Farrell paid great attention to the
   Warehouse.
Walls fed horses up to Thursday.

Arnotts still has the broken lock of the warehouse garage door mentioned on Thursday 27 April. The main worry of the writers of these reports seems to have been fear of stock losses by looting (as had occurred in Clerys and other Sackville (now O'Connell) Street stores). The sprinkler system may have reassured them about the possibility of a serious fire, but they were aware that Clerys had been destroyed. Britain Street was renamed Denmark Street and was included in the site rebuilt by Roches Stores after the Second World War.

The second document is a letter written to his sister by Arnotts' company secretary, Henry Beater, whose fears for the second destruction of the store by fire could hardly be more clearly expressed.

Friday 5th May 1916

My dear Margaret,

   Your postcard dated 27th April was delivered here
(says Alice) about 2 p.m today. On Easter Monday, the
24th April, I biked to Phoenix Park, saw hockey match,
and returned about 4.40. Noticed people in groups here
and there and some few soldiers standing near barracks,
but was not for a moment alarmed or even suspicious,
merely supposing it an idle way of spending bank
holiday. In due course I went to bed, perhaps earlier than
usual, anticipating a big post next morning. Grace came
up with Stanley's report (just returned from his outing)
that the Sinn Feiners (pronounced 'Shin Fayners' =
Gaelic meaning 'Ourselves Alone') had captured the
GPO – Westland Row, Harcourt Street, St Stephen's
Green etc. etc. Next morning I walked in to Henry
Street, no trams, overhead wires pulled down in many
places, firing across Stephen's Green and road barricaded
with motor cars. Unknown to myself I must have again

and again passed through danger zones and according to subsequent reports of multitudes of civilian deaths shot down in the very streets I went along I take it that a gracious and merciful hand protected me. Crossed the bridge into Sackville Street and saw a flag over GPO 'Irish Republic' then I began to think the tomfoolery more serious than the idiotic joke which at first I half supposed it to be, reached and entered Arnott & Co., but no business and no shops opened, the staff before 11 o'clock thoroughly frightened hurried to their homes and after our ledgers and books etc were redeposited in strong room I saw trams going and went home too. Wednesday morning still ignorant of my real danger or perhaps making little of it, once again I went to Henry St, witnessed shameful looting on all sides. Liptons & Co. emptied absolutely etc. etc. etc. Didn't enter Arnott & Co. but went home again. Thursday morning, in some degree realising my risk, I again went to Henry Street but the sight was too awful and quickly I hurried home, stopped by soldiers three times and once at Cork Hill angrily shouted down a lane out of a firing line into which I had accidentally entered. Then Rathmines became a prison. We could get no butter and once nearly ran out of bread, firing everywhere night and day. Stanley sitting in the garden heard a whiz and a bullet entered the grass at his feet – a miracle he was not shot there and then in broad day light. Then nightly fires and nightly machine guns finally came on and now Sackville Street is something like 'Ypres'. House after house destroyed utterly. Clery & Co., DBC, Eason, GPO, Metropole and Imperial Hotels, Freeman's Journal *and literally dozens of other establishments in ruins. Henry St on both sides from the pillar to Arnott & Co. nearly every house down and absolutely ruined but through the mercy of God A. & Co. alone (almost) still standing – though every window of shop front smashed two fires on premises extinguished before much damage. Yet we have suffered much – returned to business yesterday (some of us) and today Friday 5th May first day opened for trade since Easter Monday 24th April. Oswald & George &*

After the 1916 Rising: (above) the destruction of Henry Street. Arnotts just
missed the destruction – see top left corner (contemporary photograph by
T. J. Westropp, 18 May 1916, courtesy Royal Irish Academy)
(below) insurance map showing buildings totally and partially destroyed
(from *Sinn Féin Revolt Illustrated* courtesy Royal Irish Academy)

*James Hardy lost their little all at 17 Lower Sackville
Street. Hampton Leedon & Co. (Deverells) nothing left
but a ruined pile of bricks but there you must know more
than I do, or rather you knew all long before I did for we
in all the suburbs were prisoners confined to narrow
areas and obliged under martial law to be indoors at
7.30 p.m. I could go on and on writing and writing
details upon details but am too utterly disgusted the
numbers of murders and deaths is simply dreadful. No
gas yet – to be turned on at 6 p.m tomorrow. We had a
damaged goods sale today and had to shut out large
crowds – letting in batches from time to time and
business I believe will now return. 22 years ago 4th &
5th May 1894 Arnotts fire and today once again I look
on ruins thankful to God said ruins are not Arnott &
Co. – how we escaped is a wonder of wonders for the
military were in deadly earnest for days and their
artillery must have destroyed most of the many houses
now in ruins – I can say nothing more than 'astounding
mercy of God to spare A. & Co.'. Were you to walk down
Henry Street or Sackville Street and see all you'd say
impossible and how could A. & Co. escape!*

*. . . dear Maggie there can be no doubt God heard the
prayers of HWB & HDB for A. & Co. and Brown
Thomas & Co. the latter absolutely intact except a
cracked window above shop. Poor James Hardy he
prayed too and I for Hoyte & Co. but the house is no
more and all George's plans and expensive tools and
utensils lost, the damage to Dublin property is estimated
at £2,000,000 and I cannot think this figure
overvaluation in fact it looks to me rather under the
mark. A. & Co. have lost amongst other things about 10
days' trade in the very best part of our season. Our
stables and workshops burnt out. All motors gone and
horses and the houses we let to tenants to wit Nos.
16.17.21.22.23.28.50 Henry Street all in ruins. Nos. 7 &
8 damaged severely. But now we are at it again with
God's blessing. We shall yet come up again. The people
believe in us and my Directors are men of high integrity.
We have large reserves and I believe are better after*

*[able] to face trouble than any other house in Ireland and
to overcome it so cheer up and praise Him and pray for
me.*

   *Yours
       Harry.*

*Pearse the President of Irish Republic (shot) was in my
office about two years ago about his a/c.*[4]

*   *   *   *   *

During the early years of this century working conditions
for many in Dublin were hard, as described so vividly in
James Plunkett's *Strumpet City*. One can still remember the
plight of coalmen driving their horses and carts in heavy
rain with only a cap and an empty coal sack across their
shoulders for protection. Retail deliveries for Arnotts were
made up to the 1920s by 'bagmen'; an ageing and bent old
member of that order is clearly remembered making these
deliveries round houses in Dalkey. He had, of course,
travelled out by tram – fare 8d at that time. His name was
Roche and his life was cheered up in small ways by cups of
tea and occasional tips given to him by sympathetic
customers.[5]

Bagmen were not too low in the social system to have
their pride, and indeed spirit. Alexander Nesbitt told a
story about a discontented bagman who, when refused
permission to go home a little early on Christmas Eve,
threw his load of blankets into the Liffey. Not an Arnotts'
bagman we presume.

Alexander Nesbitt did not forget his origins, but he was
now management, and staff and management in Arnotts

---

[4]Pearse's account was probably for his school, St Enda's, in Rathfarnham.

[5]In the 1950s the idea of pooling deliveries by area between two
leading department stores in Dublin was proposed but the idea was too
advanced for the management of one of the stores. The bagmen had
come to this arrangement years before, in the early 1900s. They met in a
pub and re-sorted their deliveries so that each would have to cover
only one part of the city. Sometimes one wonders who is really running
things.

were bound to come to argument at some stage as staff developed, understandably, their idea of what was just. Arnotts' first strike took place in October 1918.

The Irish Union of Distributive Workers had been pressing for a meeting with the management of Arnotts but was steadily refused. Alexander Nesbitt was in his late sixties and never given to compromise, and although his second son William was co-opted a director in October 1917 on the death of William Wallace, he did not at that stage introduce any moderating influence.

A clear and balanced account of the strike appeared in the December 1918 edition of the *Draper's Assistant*.

> On the 19th October, acting on a requisition from the staff of the firm, the Executive Committee of the Association made application for an increase on present salaries at the rate of 33⅓ per cent, such increase to date from the 1st August last. The firm replied by stating that the question of increase of salaries was considered twice annually, immediately after each stock-taking; these dates being 31st July and 31st January. This reply was considered unsatisfactory, but the firm again refused to go into the matter. A further letter was sent with a similar result. They were also asked to receive a deputation from the Executive Committee to discuss the question, but the firm could not see their way to do so, consequently a deadlock arose and it was decided to send in a strike notice stating that the staff would not resume work on the morning of the 21st November unless a satisfactory reply was received. No reply came; hence the strike, and the thoroughness and order with which it was conducted is the admiration of the citizens generally. It was, in fact, 'the completest thing on record'. Not one employee out of between 400 and 450 all told entered the employment of the firm that morning. The pickets were on duty at 7 o'clock, and the other workers, who are members of several other unions, were informed of the exact position of

affairs. The pickets were, no doubt, active, but to the credit of the other workers be it said, it did not require much pressure or force to induce them to abstain from work on the occasion. The futility of endeavouring to carry on was recognised immediately by the directors, with the result that the dispute developed into a partial 'lock-out' as well as a strike; all doors were closed.

The strike was not long in operation when efforts were made towards a settlement, a number of these proving abortive. The directors were willing to allow the matter to go to arbitration of the Ministry of Labour, but this the Association refused. Through intermediaries it soon became apparent that the intervention of the Lord Mayor would be acceptable to both sides, but there was some difficulty in arranging as to the capacity in which he should be asked to act. The firm favoured arbitration; and the Association, in the absence of any offer from the firm, felt that there was nothing to arbitrate upon. Finally it was agreed that both sides would meet under the chairmanship of the Lord Mayor, all preliminaries and procedure to be discussed and arranged at that sitting. As a consequence a conference took place in the Mansion House under the chairmanship of Lord Mayor O'Neill at 4 o'clock on the evening of the 5th December. Mr A. Nesbitt, chairman and managing director of the company, represented Messrs Arnott and Co., and Miss Cahalan, Messrs J. Twomey, W. J. McNabb and M. J. O'Lehane represented the employees on behalf of our Association. After a brief discussion it was agreed that the case be gone into immediately under the chairmanship of the Lord Mayor, his lordship acting as chairman and in an advisory and intermediary capacity generally. Although the conference lasted three hours there was scarcely any hitch during the proceedings, our representatives being met in a most fair and conciliatory spirit by the representatives of the firm.

Finally it was agreed that an increase of 30 per cent be paid on present salaries, such increase to date from 1st August last; all employees to be paid one week's salary or wages during cessation of work.

It was pointed out by our representatives during negotiations that other societies who had members in the firm had put in a demand since the strike arose, and that our members could not resume work until their demands were conceded or adjusted. The Lord Mayor undertook to communicate with the unions who had made demands and to hold himself personally responsible, it being distinctly understood that we would not return to work until the matter was settled with the other unions. Being unable to arrive at an adjustment that night, it was decided that a conference of the representatives of the other societies be held the following day (Friday) at 4 o'clock, and that the firm would not re-open for the present. The conference was duly held on Friday, when a satisfactory solution was found; the porters, packers, domestic staff and motormen receiving an increase of 8s per week and one week's pay during the strike and, in the case of the other workers who put in no demand, they would receive two weeks' pay, all hands to return to work on Monday, 9th December.

The increase of 30 per cent is quite amazing and must have represented a long pent-up demand and no doubt the rapid inflation caused by the war. Buyers and managers were obviously rewarded by bonuses, if not by high salaries; at the annual general meeting of March 1918 it was mentioned that bonuses totalling £12,027 and advances of £2,965 had been paid to staff during the last three and a half years. On the suggestion of a shareholder, Robinson, seconded by another named Doyle, the increase of £2,600 in the carry-forward was added to these amounts. The rank and file had taken note.

After this defeat of management the directors decided in

January 1920 to leave the Merchant Drapers' Association but rejoined in 1921 after that body had concluded a trade-wide wage agreement. The union again served a demand in May 1922 declaring that Arnotts had not applied in principle the terms of the 1920 minimum wage agreement, and claiming in particular a bonus for the wholesale staff to make up a shortfall in rates of pay in that division; at the same time the restoration of commission to retail sales people on sales made to wholesale customers was demanded.

It looks as if the 30 per cent rise in pay in 1918 was enough to keep the retail staff happy, but had left the wholesale short. Alexander Nesbitt had also tried to trim expenses by cancelling commission on retail sales to wholesale customers. His reason would have been that these needed no selling, but this was hardly true; a wholesale customer buying retail might on average be even more particular and more prone to annul a sale by returning goods. Since profits in calendar year 1922 were normal at £24,000 he was probably preparing for a slump to follow the post-war boom. Of course it came, and in 1929 minimum rates of pay in the drapery trade in Dublin were reduced for newly-engaged staff.

The report in the *Distributive Worker* of this second strike, which secured the demands of the union, is again calm in tone but it does show both Arnotts and the Merchant Drapers' Association in an unflattering light. On this occasion the precaution was not taken to secure the position of the seven other unions in Arnotts catering for what is described as a section of the 'dressmakers, tailors, porters and a few odd workers here and there in the firm'. These demanded full wages for the days they were out because of the staff strike and one of their spokesmen admitted the claim was 'an innovation'.

This action prolonged the strike for another two weeks. Some of these other workers were members of the Distributive Workers' Union and received strike pay – this union was able to turn the account into a cautionary tale for the members of the other unions, who received, it was said, no pay while on strike; it was, declared the

Distributive Worker, 'the most serious setback in the shop life of Dublin within the last ten years'.

That Alexander behaved so insensitively in these two arguments with Arnotts staff must be put down to inexperience in the area of staff relations, probably typical of employers at that time, particularly if they tended to be dominant in personality. He was not a cold man. During one of these strikes, standing outside the store, he was warned by police to be careful. 'But these are my friends', he declared emotionally waving his hands towards the pickets. He was about seventy years of age at the time and surely puzzled by the war-changed world around him.

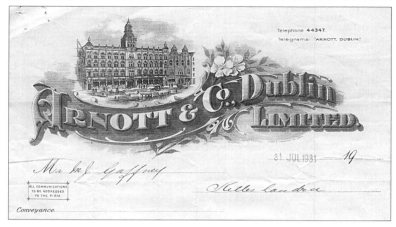

A decorative bill-head in use in the 1920s and 1930s.

A covered carriage entrance, since removed, jutting into Henry Street from the furniture department

Alexander Nesbitt after his retirement as chairman

6 TRYING TIMES 1919–1938

DURING THE First World War profits had been subject to a 100 per cent excess profits tax. It is not surprising that the profits, having been declared at £19,000 in calendar year 1914, did not exceed £25,000 until the post-war calendar year 1919! At the beginning of 1919, when the war had ended, reserves had risen to £50,000 and cash in hand, with overspill into investments, totalled £66,000. When the boom that followed the war added to these pent-up reserves, it was easy to declare a capital bonus of two for every three £4 ordinary shares, bringing the issued ordinary capital to £100,000 – thus was the fire loss more than returned to the ordinary shareholders.

In 1919 post-war bumper profits of £51,000 had to be declared, but in 1920 profits were back to £18,000. The directors reported that the first six months had been exceptional, but the second six were disappointing. When a shareholder, Doyle, said Todd Burns and Pims had increased profits, Alexander blandly resisted the implied criticism, replying that he was very glad their friendly competitors had done so well. He went on to declare that he had never been more confident in recommending the directors' report as he was that day; they had not seen the end of the slump.

In 1921 Alexander increased pressure on his buyers to mark down stocks, showing a net profit for that year of only £10,000; this enabled the auditors, Craig Gardner, to reclaim £25,000 of excess profits tax overpaid, bringing the surplus for calendar year 1921 to £35,000, with stocks, we hope, thoroughly purged.

In 1922, 'despite the interruption of business due to a

misunderstanding with staff in July', profits were back to a prudent £24,000; and the chairman was able to announce with obvious pride that the item 'goodwill' of £53,000 had been completely written off.

Thus, in his seventieth year, boosted by his skilful management of the post-war boom, Alexander Nesbitt had succeeded in his overriding aim of strengthening the company financially. He had, however, lost touch with his staff. From that loss of touch stemmed his greatest failure: he had not trained a successor in management.

The First World War changed society so profoundly that there was some excuse for the failure of a man in advanced middle age to adapt. Everything changed, inwardly as well as outwardly, the position of women in particular, but also women's fashions in dress, furnishing, houses, relations between classes, methods of transport and communication.

The photo-montage of some of Arnotts' senior staff in 1907 shows 67 men and 10 women (see pages 52-3); most of the men still had moustaches and all had stiff high wing or starched collars; the women invariably had long hair pinned up on top of or behind their heads and wore high-necked blouses or dresses. After the war, the new freedom for women was expressed in their looser, shorter, simpler style of dress, which to this day at its best shows the influence of that wonderful French designer Coco Chanel.

The war had brought women to the staff in greater numbers and in greater prominence. Miss Cahalan of Arnotts became president of the Distributive Workers' Union in 1922 and the setting up of the shirt factory in Arnotts in 1921 had added greatly to the number of women employed.

At this time, Alexander must have felt under pressure. Sales had peaked in 1920 at £933,000, due mainly to the post-war boom in the wholesale side but were down to around £600,000 in 1925, when he finally persuaded his second son, William, to take over the management of the company.

To effect this change of management Alexander brought William into Arnotts one morning, introduced him very briefly to each of the managers and buyers and then said,

'Well, I'll be off now.' Apart from board and annual general meetings Alexander hardly showed himself in Arnotts again. Chairing these meetings he aimed to keep them as short as possible.

William, who was forty years of age at the time, had started work in London in 1901, on the day of Queen Victoria's funeral. His employer was the Mazawattee Tea Company, and his boss John Lane Densham, whom he admired for his interest in the manufacture of bicycles. William was, in economic theory, a sort of latter day physiocrat, believing that wealth consisted in the production of food and raw materials, and their manufacture into goods; he did not credit distribution with adding value, and would not have agreed with the opinion of the trader in Moore Street that 'in hell water would be worth sixpence a glass'.

In 1907, Alexander had bought a run-down tobacco factory, Wm Ruddell, for William to manage when he had tired of trying to sell tea around the eastern counties of England. Protesting that he knew nothing about tobacco, William was lucky enough to find an excellent factory manager already working in Ruddells; in partnership with him William provided the sales and financial management needed to make a considerable success of the business by 1922.

It is not surprising that William was unwilling to devote himself to managing Arnotts, regarding much of that business as work for women. But he did as his father wished, taking a cut in earnings in the change: Alexander kept part of his salary as a pension and did not wish their joint pay to cost the company more.

William was Alexander's second son and either did not regard himself as academic, or thought his role should be to earn some money instead of prolonging his education. His elder brother, George, had qualified as a physician, with an address in St Stephen's Green and an attachment to Richmond Hospital. He acted for some years as medical officer to Arnotts for which he was paid £100 a year.

The third and fourth brothers were Alexander (Alec) a qualified engineer who served in France as a major in the

Staff outing to Bettystown July 1937

British Army and Robert (Roy) a doctor who joined the Royal Navy, achieved the rank of surgeon-commander and was killed on board his ship in Alexandria in 1942 during a German air attack. The youngest of the five was Sydney, a very young dispatch rider in France in 1918, who took over the management of Ruddells, the tobacco factory, after William's departure to Arnotts.

Alexander had turned the job of managing Arnotts into a lonely one by gathering all authority into his own hands as chairman and managing director; twenty years earlier, the chairman had retail and wholesale managing directors in his team. Until the Second World War no one else in Arnotts was given the title of manager, although titles do not always cost much. William Nesbitt was 'The Manager' – that was, as it were, the first commandment. Every other member of staff with responsibility for managing was called simply Mr, Miss or Mrs.

Mr Jack Worrall of the parcel office was really the manager of deliveries and transport, a formidable task in which even that honest, blunt-spoken man earned respect as well as some degree of unpopularity in proving that the job was being fairly and economically done. He is believed to have run away from home at the age of thirteen and started work in Arnotts in 1894, living in. He married in 1918, 'from stock' as the saying in Arnotts goes, Isobel (Bel) Hume, the typist to the company secretary.

Worrall's son, Leslie, joined Arnotts' staff in 1936, taken from school before sitting the Intermediate Certificate because of the terminal illness of his father. He rose to the position of chief cashier and his patience and invariable good humour made him certainly most popular, though cashiers have been known for their crustiness.

Trading managers were, of course, called buyers, and shop supervisors were called superintendents; travellers – peripatetic salesmen – were very big men, especially in the wholesale trade; but there was only one Manager.

William certainly had the necessary energy and patience and was financially astute, but he had little office back-up. To two decimal places everything was worked out on the back of an envelope – a used envelope, of course; he was

devoted to economy in everything except expenditure of
his own time. He started his period as manager with an
ageing directorate and had little luck in recruiting new
members to the board. George Collins died in April 1926,
after nineteen years of service, leaving the directors five in
number, the minimum required at that time by the articles.
They were: Alexander Nesbitt, chairman, O. P. Beater,
William Wallace, James Cooke and William Nesbitt.

In June 1929, O. P. Beater died, aged eighty-one, after
thirty-seven years' service. Laurence Howard, buyer of the
main departments for women's outerwear such as 'mantles,
costumes and furs' was co-opted to fill the vacant place. His
early death in the following year was reported to the annual
general meeting of March 1931 by chairman Alexander as
follows: 'Mr Howard's period of office was very short; he
attended only one general meeting, but he had been with
the firm for twelve years, and will always be remembered as
a most agreeable, capable and unassuming man.'[1]

Howard's co-option had been a belated response to a
suggestion by shareholders in 1924 that some senior
members of the staff be put on the board. His place was
taken by Patrick J. O'Neill as a non-executive director. But
the following year William Wallace died; he was replaced
by Major Alec Nesbitt who had returned to live in Dublin
after some years of working in South America and Siam;
he had advised the company as consultant engineer for
some years. The resignation of Patrick J. O'Neill in 1935,
owing to ill-health, was not taken as an opportunity to
import new talent to the board; possibly for reasons of
economy the company secretary, Fortescue Monsell, was
co-opted.

---

[1] In the 1930s Howard's son Reginald succeeded him as buyer of
mantles (retail coats), cloaks (wholesale coats) and cashmeres (lighter
woollen materials). Reginald later became a floor manager. He had
very long service in Arnotts because he neither wished nor could afford
to retire: he had married late, and his wife died young, leaving a family
of whom the eldest was thirteen. That the family survived and
succeeded is a tribute to this very patient man whose tolerance and
understanding helped so greatly to preserve the peace on the main
floor of Arnotts.

Monsell had succeeded that estimable, invaluable and long-serving scribe, Henry Beater, who died in 1933. Henry had filled in the figures for the first half of that year in the black, leather-bound book lettered in gold 'Chairman's Private Figures', and had entered the dates up to 1937 to take the figures of the future. But Monsell did not continue to use the book, which records sales from 1856 and other figures from 1894.

The death of James Cooke on 24 February 1939, just before the annual general meeting which reported the year 1938, with possibly the least satisfactory-looking set of figures in the company's history to that date, left the directorate flying on one wing.

William Nesbitt had taken over as managing director at a challenging time. How would Arnott's fare in the new Irish Free State?

The answer proved to be 'better than expected'. It was not the government and certainly not the British-trained civil service that failed the new state, it was general economic depression from 1923. Agricultural prices fell, compounded by the shock of the return of Britain and Northern Ireland, and with them the Irish Free State, to the gold standard in 1926. Until 1931, when the gold standard was abandoned in conditions of major slump, activity and prices were severely affected.[2] The Irish consumer price index, base 100 in July 1914, fell from an annual average of 188 in 1922 to 160 in 1931.

The index bottomed out in 1933 at 151, a post-war fall of 20 per cent. Between 1927 and 1932 the important agricultural price index fell from 132.9 to 108.7. A silent revolution had taken place in Irish agriculture between 1911 and 1936 – the number of agricultural labourers halved in that period.

In 1923 the directors decided to continue to meet fortnightly, which suggests their uncertainty about the

---

[2]Seen from the author's viewpoint, that of a boy at an English boarding school from 1927 to 1931, the price of his weekly one pound jar of Hartley's marmalade came down from 9d to 6½d.

future. On the other hand, to show their confidence, in November they invested £20,000 in the new National Loan. This earned a letter of appreciation from the Minister for Finance. Despite forebodings, sales did not fall below £600,000, or profits below £20,000, until the 1930s.

The fall of 50 per cent in wholesale sales after the post-war peak was more severe than the fall of 26 per cent in retail sales – the latter should have been the more profitable, but since wholesale and retail trading were combined in each department in the same account at a gross profit averaging over 17 per cent on sales, it was difficult to be precise about where profits were made.

Judging from the Manager's actions, the main attack was concentrated on expenses. The ceilings of the shop had been painted in 1924 – this did not happen again until 1948. 'Women never look up' was William's dictum. Staff numbers were reduced. Superintendent David Swords, an imposing figure with magnificent beard and frock coat, whose flourish when placing the old, uncomfortable, bent-wood chairs for lady customers was unmatched, was retired with a pension of £250 from the benevolent fund. Joseph V. Martin, with service since 1878, retired with a pension of £200. In 1926 a risky attempt at terminating the employment of Miss Cahalan (Mrs Burns), an active member of the Distributive Workers' Union, on the grounds that she was a married woman, was not concluded. The minute 'married and should leave' has been crossed out of the board minute book.

In August 1926, Miss D. Arthur, Miss McRory and Miss R. Kennedy retired on pensions of £110, £100 and £75 respectively; Miss Kennedy, who was in the millinery department, sent the directors a gracious letter of thanks. She and Miss Arthur feature in the photo-montage of senior staff of 1907, both handsome women possibly in their early fifties at that time.

By the end of 1932, when total sales had sunk to around £500,000 and net profits to £15,000, William Nesbitt had reduced the dividend proposed on the ordinary shares to 6¼ per cent in steps from the 11¼ per cent paid in the last years of the 1920s. Despite the strong financial position he must have felt uncertain of the future. He had good reason. The first Fianna Fáil government had come into power in the spring and had at once introduced a high tariff policy for imported goods. In June, the land annuities were withheld, and the Economic War began. By the time William presented his report, agricultural prices had dropped to 1914 levels.

Another attempt was made to terminate the employment of Miss Cahalan, who had, as we have seen, been prominent in the affairs of the Distributive Workers' Union and was felt by management to be a very troublesome member of staff, and of a Mrs Young. The result was a strike on 22 November 1932 by staff who were members of the Distributive Workers' Union, about 300 workers in all; this figure included sales staff, clerical staff, tailors, workroom and factory hands; no members of the Irish Transport and General Workers' Union were involved. The strike was settled by paying nine months' earnings to the two women instead of the three months' offered and promising to consider a contributory pension scheme. Arnotts agreed on the understanding that the right of the company to 'adjust staff' as considered necessary was admitted.

Arnotts had rejoined the Merchant Drapers' Association in 1921 but refused at this time an offer of sympathetic action, presumably a lock-out, by the Association owing to the 'great hardship and suffering that would be caused to the many workers who would be involved'. Looking back, it seems extraordinary that some other employers in the Association (not all by any means) would take action, at cost to themselves and their staff, to maintain some stated principle, such as the right of management to dismiss staff. (We shall see that some years later owners of drapery shops at times shouted for action by the employers' group to help settle some staff problem, but it was very rare to find help offered by the group.)

The negotiations, conducted on behalf of Arnotts by Robert J. Kidney, secretary of the Merchant Drapers' Association, and two members of his committee well-disposed to Arnotts, David Kellett and Wesley Hanna,

Pickets politely parading in the rain: the strike of 1932

Four Nesbitts and their wives flanked by members of the dance committee, photographed at the Metropole in the early 1930s. Alexander Nesbitt is standing fourth from left, Mrs Sydney Nesbitt is between him and William, Major Alec is on the far right of that row, and Sydney is behind his own wife.

secretary of Switzers, were referred for arbitration of a senior official of the Department of Industry and Commerce. The correspondence is confused and the procedure seems cumbersome today. Robert Kidney is remembered as a polite and kindly man whose ability qualified him for more rewarding tasks than conducting the quarrels of self-righteous drapers. 'Self-righteous' because the minutes of Arnotts' board meeting state: 'The company must hold firmly to its right to be judge of what alterations in the staff were necessary in the efficient conduct of the business, and without necessarily assigning any reason.' The tone, which was William Nesbitt's, was softened in a letter he wrote to the arbitrator: 'I have been asked by the Chairman to add that as the Father, in years, of the whole staff, he deplores any difference; and he is determined while he lives no injustice will be done to any of them.'

The proposed trade-wide pension scheme for members of the Distributive Workers' Union was later occasionally raised but never came to fruition. But in 1938 Arnotts' board decided on a pension scheme for staff – this was Alexander's idea, rather than William's, but as usual William, who believed that everyone should save for old age, did what his father wished; Alexander had after all started at the bottom, and to the end did not forget what that meant.

Poor economic conditions were not the only troubles of Arnotts' management in the early 1930s. By 1933 the Fianna Fáil protective tariffs began to bite. Clothing generally was subjected to 60 per cent. This altered completely the existing relationship of Arnotts' buyers of clothing with, for example, suppliers in London. Before, it had been possible to telephone an order for a particular size and colour to London, have the parcel put on the Irish Mail overnight, and open it in Dublin the following morning.

Import duties and quotas, with which Arnotts learnt to live for the following forty years, created a new type of office employment, that of customs clerk – much as today's increasing lawlessness has promoted the employment of security staff.

On top of these difficulties for traders came the depressing effect of the Economic War with Britain from 1932 to 1938.

Attending Arnotts' splendid staff dances in the early 1930s in the Metropole Ballroom, with the men not merely in dinner jackets but often in tails and the women impressively ball-gowned, one would never have suspected the undercurrents and trials of those times. The Nesbitt family attended in force, even old Alexander and his wife, Elizabeth; in the late 1930s the O'Connors and Fagans embellished further the attendant directorate.

The chairman told the annual general meeting in March 1933: 'I think we ought to be satisfied that the report is as good as it is having regard to the state of trade in the country. The balance sheet shows a very strong financial position, we have plenty of cash in hand, and taking advantage of this we have installed up to date fixtures and fittings throughout the shop.'

These fittings were manufactured by Sage of London for whom Patrick J. O'Connor was agent, before he formed his own shopfitting business, O'Connor & Bailey; he was of great help to William Nesbitt in his first attempts to bring the store up to date.

William was attempting in conditions of difficulty and change to give Arnotts a renewed impetus. Though he must have know the retail trade was the sure source of profits, at heart he was a manufacturer and wholesaler; he considered wholesaling more difficult than retailing (and therefore more meritorious), because the trader had to go out to find the customers. Besides, the new government's economic policy called for import substitution at the very least and in the 1930s Arnotts had unused space.

In a burst of activity around 1935, William opened a workroom in buildings on the other side of Prince's Street for manufacturing women's dresses. Registered as Women's Wear Ltd., the enterprise sold only to wholesalers, to Arnotts' wholesale and its wholesale competitors. This plunge into manufacturing dresses for the wholesale trade was a surprising misfit in any logical view of Arnotts' organisation – it probably resulted from the chance finding of a factory manager who knew that particular trade.

A much more useful manufacturing unit, again registered as a wholly-owned subsidiary, this time under the name Milne Models Ltd, was set up on the top floor in Henry Street in vacant space which may have been built to house staff and was never used for that purpose. The first manageress was called Milne (always pronounced 'Milney' in the southern part of the country) who produced hand veined blouses for sale to retail stores including, of course, Arnotts retail. The unit was turned over to making women's dresses in 1938 and flourished during and after the Second World War under the management of the energetic Margaret (Peggy) Forkan.

But what proved to be a much larger effort was the opening, again in the buildings off Prince's Street, of Irish Textiles Ltd for the manufacture of knitwear. This company was financed and owned by William Nesbitt in partnership with the McDevitt family of Glenties, Co. Donegal – it simply rented space from Arnotts until it built a factory off East Wall Road. During the Second World War and after it proved to be a very useful supplier to the retail trade under the brand name 'Highland'. It was managed by William's younger son, Alexander (Alec junior).

But Arnotts' retail was provided for more directly too, by the opening in 1937 of what was called a café, meant to be modelled on Bewleys Cafés, but which turned out to be a restaurant because its organising consultants, the Ulster Menu Company, were restaurateurs. This was planned to cost £5,000 but, fully equipped, cost nearly twice that amount. It was from the start, and has been ever since in its successive metamorphoses, an outstanding success.

In 1937, impressed by the developing speciality of advertising, and with his loyal business friend, Harry Jauncey of the Temple Press, William opened and financed an advertising agency, Janus Ltd. The agency, managed by Reginald Wilks, was intended to produce 'good' advertising for Arnotts and other clients. Wilks, who came from England though he had an Irish background, was quietly spoken, methodical, immensely hardworking, patient and pleasant – he set Janus on its feet.[3]

On the day of a rugby international in 1939 Reginald Wilks was attacked by a group of men after nightfall near his hotel on the seafront at Dun Laoghaire. They were thought to have intended to tar and feather him. He clung to railings and, shouting for help, attracted the attention of some passers-by. After injuring one of Wilks's hands with some blunt instrument in trying to drag him from the railings, the men ran off.

Poor Wilks had his hand bandaged and in a sling for some weeks and for quite a while afterwards was accompanied on all his comings and goings by an armed plain-clothes policeman. Wilks's *sang-froid* survived this attack. There were minor compensations such as his *succés fou* at a party for young people which he attended complete with bodyguard. One of Arnotts' buyers, Thomas Ryan, was accused by the police of organising the attack. The directors suspended him until his name was cleared by his acquittal, to the delight of his friends in Arnotts; William Nesbitt made a point of attending at the court to shake his hand.

The 1930s was a turbulent time. The Economic War, coming on top of the dislocation to trading caused by the government's economic policy, kept Arnotts' retail sales relatively thin. However, wholesale sales were boosted somewhat during that period by the increased difficulty of obtaining and financing supplies, and possibly also by the appointment of William McCormack, formerly employed by Pim Brothers, as wholesale traveller in Dublin district. Until then there had been five travellers, Tim Brosnan, Jim Freely, John

---

[3]After the outbreak of war in September 1939, Reginald Wilks dutifully returned to England. A surprisingly young Denis Garvey was entrusted with Janus's future development. In this he was very successful. The agency passed through its hands to promotion in the growing trade of advertising quite a number of talented young people; on the way it did some excellent award-winning work for Arnotts and other accounts. In the 1960s the non-executive shareholding was sold to Denis Garvey and the other managers leaving them also in possession of the house they occupied in Parnell Square.

Heskins, Willie McGreevy and Dick Murphy covering rather peculiarly-drawn journeys round the country outside Dublin. When William asked Alexander's opinion of the proposed appointment he received the usual 'encouraging' Nesbitt parental reply: 'Try it if you like, my boy, but it won't do any good.' It became in due course a decided success.

In Arnotts, the 1930s seem to have been filled with management's attempts to re-establish control. William must have felt saddled with what seemed the Herculean labour of moving the cumbersome show firmly into the middle of the twentieth century. One particular uncertainty did cloud management's outlook: in most departments it could not distinguish the profits of retail trading from profits of wholesale trading, because the two trades were combined in one trading account.[4]

At the beginning of the 1930s retail and wholesale trading was separated in only one type of stock – women's underwear was split into underclothing (wholesale) and lingerie (retail). At that time it was usual to have net losses of profit in perhaps half-a-dozen departments each half year. By 1938, wholesale trading accounts had been separated from their retail counterparts in another six departments.

This separation did not necessarily increase sales, but it did reveal the more profitable nature of the retail trading.[5] The only departments to achieve noticeably increased sales

---

[4]Stocks were held in the departments' accounts at cost to which was added the cost of incoming goods as invoices were passed by the buyer, and from which sales less 16⅔ per cent were deducted, leaving the remaining stocks theoretically at cost price. If the rate of 16⅔ per cent was less than the real margin, as in the case of millinery, the book stock was over-credited and extra gross profit emerged at the half-yearly stock-taking on 31 July and 31 January, but on the other hand if price reductions to dispose of goods brought the average margin below 16⅔ per cent, the stock turned out short by the books and showed less than expected gross profit.

[5]In the autumn half of 1938, out of 29 departments 15 with mainly retail trade showed surplus gross profits amounting in most cases to between 5 and 10 per cent of sales, whereas eight departments trading only by wholesale showed small shortages of profit (or exceptionally one large shortage) which revealed trading at less than the margin of 16⅔. The remaining six largely retail departments came out roughly as expected with a gross profit of about 17 per cent.

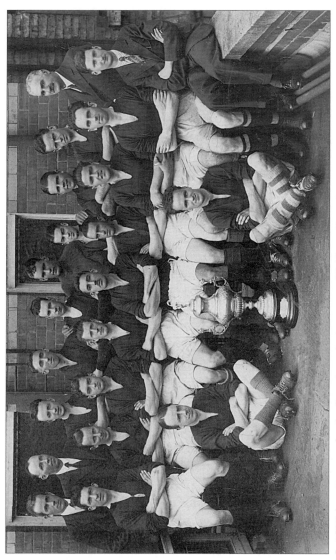

In 1935 Arnotts won, for the first time, the inter-store Kickham Cup:
(back, left to right) W. McSorley, J. Leahy, R. Murray, T. Purcell, P. Flood, T. Hickey, E. Langan, F. Dowds, B. Ryan, Mr Downes
(middle, left to right) P. Murphy, A. McGinty, T. Langan, G. Coyle, M. O'Kane, J. Bracken, M. Delany, J. Thompson, B. Liddy
(front, left to right) T. Gorevan, T. McLernon.

in the 1930s were hosiery under Thomas Hallinan and linens under Hugh Neary. This is not surprising when we hear tales from that time showing that most buyers did not expect trade to increase in normal circumstances – in fact one or two closed their books with the remark 'I've done my trade' a week or two before the half-year was over. No further new goods were opened before stock-taking and in one case junior staff played a type of football behind improvised curtains.

A buyer could make a gross profit that seemed too large to be believed or more often too small. When asked for an explanation the vaguest generalisations about poor weather (in clothing departments) or poor trade were offered. Management could only say 'Let's hope you do better this season'; any other remedy involved removing that buyer from the job.

The task of organising a new system of stock control was one beyond the limited resources of Arnotts' existing office staff. In January 1939, therefore, Reginald Wilks, whose patience fitted him for the task, had been asked to under-take this. Based on a system developed in London he designed all the books and dockets needed and the new method was put to work.[6] Though many of the frills were

---

[6]Stocks were held at selling price instead of cost. Buyers had to mark their department's invoices with the prices at which they intended to offer goods for sale so that, having at one stock-taking listed the remaining stocks at cost and selling, it was possible to add incoming stocks at cost and selling to produce an average percentage of margin at which the department was attempting to trade. This margin could be applied to sales from month to month to produce, after adjustments for any reduction in price, a gross profit for the period. Comparing the direct expenses of the department with its gross profit would then give its 'contribution' towards general overheads, and so an estimated net profit monthly.

Finally, stocks remaining after the Sales in July and January were listed at selling price and should have matched the stocks recorded at selling price in the office. To obtain stocks at cost for our accountants and auditors the average margins on sales were applied to bring the stocks to cost. The senior partner from Craig Gardner in charge of Arnotts' audit took far too long to accept this system; finally in 1944 it was admitted to be remarkably accurate.

quickly dropped by the author to avoid unnecessary criticism, it has ever since been the rock on which Arnotts' control of profitability is based.

By 1939 a total of fourteen wholesale departments had been separated in the accounts. This separation brought the promotion of women to buyer positions in the retail departments. In 1930 out of eighteen buyers the only woman was the formidable Miss Coyne, by 1940 there were four women buyers out of 27. Until the appointment of a woman to buy retail hats, they were bought by Thomas McManus along with his wholesale millinery; he wore a wig, but perhaps that was in some way a qualification – he wore a hat as well.

Profits, however, became thinner still and stocks at year end increased from around £70,000 to £93,000 in January 1938. The Economic War over, William remembered the medicine swallowed at the end of the post-1918 boom and urged buyers to take a very prudent view in their stock valuations. The result in July 1938 was a net loss of £1,235 for that first half-year and a profit of a mere £504 for the year 1938 as a whole. The report for the year to January 1939 was a dismal one, including two minor strikes and the death of director James Cooke, who had been a board member for twenty-four years. Alexander had finally been replaced as chairman by William Nesbitt, who had decided not to pay the interim dividend in July 1938; in his speech as chairman to the annual general meeting on 28 February 1939 William referred to

> the increasing importance of fashion in most of the goods we handle – and the rapid changes in fashions with the added liability of stock losses. These factors greatly increased the importance of sound stock management; and most large stores have found that a much closer control has become necessary.
>
> But the last few years of economic development have raised additional problems in this country. Restrictions on the importation of so many goods and the difficulty of obtaining suitable supplies

from Irish sources, unless orders were placed well in advance, has led, in the last year or two, to our holding much larger stocks than I certainly consider desirable. Possibly this was accentuated by the high-class nature of our business. I think that to some extent our system failed to keep our buyers in close enough touch with their requirements during this period, but this is being remedied and we should be capable of solving such problems in the future. In the year under review we experienced first a fall in prices, then a considerable hold-up in our wholesale trade before the signing of the Anglo-Irish trade agreement. In the circumstances I pressed for the reduction of stocks. This last year may well be regarded as abnormal.

The interim dividend of 2s in July was not paid; this reduced payment for the year to 5 per cent. To paraphrase the story of Albert and the Lion: 'You could see that the shareholders didn't like it.'

7 FROM ECONOMIC INTO
WORLD WAR 1939

THE DISCONTENT OF leading shareholders at the outcome of trading in 1938, their confidence shaken by the
reduction of the dividend, despite ample reserves with
which to maintain it, led to their asking one of their
members, James Fagan (Senior), to discuss the situation
with the chairman. The death of director James Cooke
within ten days of the 1939 annual general meeting
pointed the way to the resolution of the situation. Since
Alexander Nesbitt had not been able to attend the meeting,
the directorate was effectively reduced to three; the co-
option of Patrick J. O'Connor and of James Fagan in quick
succession in March 1939 restored the board to an active
five.

The contribution of the two new directors to the successful management of Arnotts was to show itself increasingly
over their years of service, but they might have been
forgiven for thinking it was immediate. It was, instead, the
outbreak of the Second World War in September 1939 that
caused Arnotts' sales, almost entirely in wholesale trade, to
rise from just over £600,000 to almost £750,000. The declared
net profits of the year 1939 at slightly above 'normal' failed
to reflect this rise in sales. The only hint was, in the Nesbitt
tradition, the addition of the words 'and other contin-
gencies' to the regular rigmarole which accompanied the
declaration of net profits. Things did look very uncertain for
business. It seemed quite possible Arnotts would, in a
prolonged war, run out of goods to sell. The First World
War had been expected to end by the first Christmas, yet it
lasted four years; would this war last longer, say six years?
This thought, believe it or not, was expressed at the time.

The chairman's speech to the general meeting of March 1940 was calculated to rally the troops; the results did not, as he claimed, 'justify the unpleasant decisions we had to take' in 1938, but his speech did stress correctly the measures he had taken to keep the company financially strong, improve its trading and organise supplies of goods in the difficult conditions of the 1930s.

Not mentioned was a strike in September 1939 lasting more than three weeks by staff members of the Distributive Workers' Union. This was caused by another attempt to dismiss a member of staff, in this case the buyer of furnishing materials, Edward Ronayne. The furnishings department had been showing a loss and he was dismissed in August 1939 with three months' salary.

From the point of view of management at that time this was justified by the vital importance of the buyer's position as trader. All members of staff were asked to sign agreements which included termination without notice. This form of agreement was challenged in court subsequently as 'harsh and unconscionable' but was upheld as 'strict certainly, but not unconscionable'.[1]

Naturally, protection of members' employment was one of the aims of the union, and Ronayne, as in the earlier case of Miss Cahalan, was in good standing with his fellow members. The decision was seen by the staff as attacking their security and two weeks' notice of withdrawal of labour was promptly given.

The author has a vivid memory of members of the house committee running rapidly around the store on Saturday 2 September 1939, shouting 'Out! Out! All out!' Poor William Flusk, a very handsome young man in the photograph of 1907, but by 1939 nervous, well on in his sixties, was fussing to complete the boxing of a woman's coat for delivery, when

---

[1]The principle of the right of management to dismiss buyers led to a larger strike in Switzers in the 1940s. Like all principles it could in practice be harsh and unreasonable; it has been replaced by the development of humane laws of employment in the 1980s, based on reasonable conditions of contract.

he was himself dispatched from his department into the street.[2]

Staff returned to work on 28 September after some buyers and superintendents had persuaded William Nesbitt to offer Edward Ronayne 'alternative employment' as a wholesale traveller. After a couple of years Ronayne left to join the Dublin Woollen Company beside the Metal Bridge.

A below-stairs story of this strike comes from James Murphy who had been engaged in 1936 as a junior boy aged fourteen.

> During this strike with the assistants and clerks the transport section was not involved. They were waiting in the engine room for their wages and wondering what was going to happen, when Mr William Nesbitt arrived carrying three large earthenware bowls containing pounds, shillings and pence. He then produced the list of names, called each person and paid each from the bowls accordingly.

That was the last strike by members of Arnotts' main union of distributive workers and clerks, now known as IDATU. Rules made by the union in the 1920s and 1930s had been extraordinarily restrictive. Everyone in the employment of the business, except directors and members of their families and a confidential secretary, had to be members of the union so all managers at any level had to be members. Buyers in the drapery trade met as a separate branch and occasionally raised questions of interest only to themselves. It was generally thought by employers that this tied the buyers (departmental managers) into a cohesive front against the directorate of the company. It did not, if these managers were devoted to their departments and to the

---

[2]Cattlemen used to call in to Arnotts, after attending the market in the North Circular Road, to buy coats for their wives; Flusk knew exactly what was required. Any doubt about size was settled when the cattleman's practised eye ran over the saleswomen in the coat department.

health of the business as a whole, and if they approved of the direction of the company. On every occasion of strike or trouble with staff in Arnotts a group of managers organised attempts to settle the problem without delay. On at least one occasion department managers, when informed by the union secretary that they were not to vote with the rank and file, insisted on their right as union members to do so.

Management in Arnotts came to see clearly, some years later, the futility of fighting with staff. A strike came to be considered a failure of management, sometimes perhaps unavoidable, but a failure nevertheless, since it destroys the confidence of staff in management. The slow task of rebuilding trust between those engaged day by day in the enterprise must then begin anew.

The author, William Nesbitt's elder son, joined Arnotts in January 1937 after spending a year in a leading advertising agency in London – the one described by Dorothy L. Sayers in her detective novel *Murder Must Advertise*. William allotted him, as usual without definite title of manager, the role of sales 'promotion' in Arnotts. This rather wide remit led in November 1938 to a 'round robin' request to the directors to receive a deputation from the staff. The directors asked for notice of the items to be discussed and deputed 'the Manager' and the company secretary to meet the delegation, which included the secretary of Arnotts' house committee, Harry Healy, and some of the livelier younger spirits such as George Towers (later chief cashier) and Harry Dillon (who developed into a wonderful display manager).

The matter for discussion was a complaint that the author and William McCormack were threatening 'to ruin the company'. It was known that the author was, apart from his other activities, planning a stock control system (discussed in Chapter 6) and Billy McCormack was the confidant of the Manager. McCormack was actually very circumspect in supplying information about the wholesale trading but he was, of course, suspected of carrying tales. Nothing came of this meeting with staff because it was clearly inspired by little more than suspicion, particularly of the new stock control system. Perhaps the new system's title, including the ambiguous word 'control', might have been more tactfully chosen.

The high import duties imposed in the 1930s had helped the development of the clothing industry in Dublin and Cork since it was a trade relatively easy to enter. By 1939 it was possible for Arnotts to find at least one Irish maker of clothing to the highest standard, but in some cases only one. Steady expansion of sales of ready-to-wear clothing was expected by Arnotts. For this trade new departments were created which were essentially new selling teams.

In 1937 a department, Inex, selling less expensive dresses made by Arnotts' dress factory, Milne Models, was opened for a new buyer, Miss Braiden; in her first year she had sales of £5,000 to add to the trade of £11,000 in the frocks department under the unique Miss Coyne. In February 1939 Eithne Murphy was appointed buyer of retail millinery; she was a good looking woman who had been used as a photographic model for some of our early advertisements for hats. In William Nesbitt's opinion this was enough to 'turn the head' of any young member of staff but it did not spoil Eithne Murphy who developed a profitable trade until it got beyond her 'control', when she had bought a wonderful stock of hats such as 'Scotts Classics' with a total selling price of over £100,000 in today's terms. But her hats were at least up to date, unlike those which were rumoured to have been in stock with another well-known wholesaler since before the First World War; those packages were never opened but solemnly counted and included year by year.

The remaining pre-Second World War developments were concerned with advertising, window display and the training of younger staff. Although less than one per cent of sales was spent on newspaper advertising in *The Irish Times*, *Independent* and *Irish Press*, or alternatively for some goods in the *Evening Herald* and *Evening Mail*, it was possible with this modest amount, using mostly six inch single or eight inch double column advertisements, to cover the greater part of Arnotts' women's and men's clothing. For a number of years the main selling seasons for fashion – March to early June and September to early

November – saw the publication of about five advertisements a week; the larger advertisements, including usually
an eleven inch treble for an event such as Fashion Week,
featured women's outerwear, and the smaller were used
for special series such as 'fitting comes first' for women's
corsetry or for men's tailoring. Arnotts wished to develop
'niche' markets in these areas; this is an ideal strategy for a
department store because it entails a larger investment and
a more skilled staff than most shops wish to maintain.

All important is the image created by the total effect of
such publicity. Janus created a logo, 'Arnotts', based on a
free-hand brush drawing of Bodoni ultra bold type, which
has been preserved to this day.

Arnotts' logo and the clean layout of its advertising were
intended to create an aura of style. The problem at first was
to imagine how everything Arnotts sold could be presented
in this light. How could women who bought our most
elegant clothes wish to live in surroundings like those of
our furniture department where dressing tables were lined
up like gravestones? This problem was solved by Cornelius
O'Shea, appointed furniture buyer in 1957.

The early argument in favour of 'good' advertising and
'good' display was that the advertising should persuade
the reader to come to Henry Street to the store; window
display should draw the shopper in Henry Street into the
store; display in the departments should do justice to the
style of goods or at least arrange them in a way and order
which made it easiest for the customer to choose. When
offered advertising buyers usually said 'Well, thank you
but could you give me more windows?' They were
deciding correctly on the promotion which suited their
stock, which had been chosen for window and department
display to the market on their doorstep; for newspaper
advertising the choice of goods would have to be more
carefully targeted and larger quantities held in stock or
available rapidly.

At that time buyers also learnt increasingly to accept
'improved' window display. In 1937 Arnotts' ten windows in
Henry Street had no backs so one could look straight
through the display into the store itself thus reducing the

William Nesbitt and members of the dance committee at a staff dance in the late 1940s (2nd row, seated from left): Ella Nesbitt, Major Alec Nesbitt, Mrs Patrick O'Connor, William Nesbitt, Agnes Nesbitt, Patrick O'Connor, Mrs Alec Nesbitt, Larry O'Dwyer.

impact of the display. The ceilings also were too high, none being lower than the front part of the store. Henry (Harry) Dillon, who was in the retail section of the cashmere department and had shown an aptitude for display draping, was picked to act as display manager. He had to give each window a 'back' by draping material across it before he started on the display of goods themselves. He needed little encouragement to have the windows backed about ten feet from the glass front by 'beaverboard', and have pelmets of the same material suspended across the top of each window to reduce it to a more comfortable height. All this board was painted white. This gave space to treat each window like a stage, with ten feet of depth to allow for backdrop separately lit.

Harry Dillon was in every sense an artist at display. An intellectual driven by his sense of design to brilliant solutions of the problems involved, he would loyally attempt to carry out display ideas suggested to him, but none was ever realised as brilliantly as the ideas he dreamed up himself.

Harold Douglas, chairman for many years of the Greenmount and Boyne Linen Company, a man with wide sympathies and many interests including a drapery store in Wexford Street, asked of Arnotts' display as managed by Dillon, 'I'm glad to see someone in Dublin doing display like that, but does it pay?'

Our buyers were not prepared to declare that it did not pay; they continued to ask for more, only arguing at times against reductions in the number of garments or goods shown. Should it not be seven, or even nine, instead of five?

Display in the departments was not very developed. One hoped some member of the sales staff 'had a taste for' display and would undertake this work. Not much space was given to display in any case; buyers preferred to fill their space with stock. At the time only the floor of 9 to 15 Henry Street, stretching back to Prince's Street, was used for the retail store and large spaces of that were taken up by linen and furnishing departments. Of the original narrow balconies along the sides of the 1898 building (extended to the next line of pillars after the war) only one was used for furniture, the other remained for some years occupied by the wholesale trimmings department, perhaps because its number of transactions made it more like a retail department.

The population of Dublin (which now included the townships) was increasing and reached a figure of 450,000 by the end of the 1930s. Arnotts' management noted that the majority of deliveries by van went to houses south of the Liffey and wondered whether Alexander Nesbitt's policy of early closing on Saturday rather than Wednesday had caused a geographical imbalance in our trading.

A creative development was the starting of tea-time fashion parades in 1938 with invitations sent to credit account customers. For many years each March and September, the parades, held in the café, were the highlights of the advertised Fashion Weeks. Over a hundred garments were shown, drawn as widely as possible from women's outerwear and indeed underwear departments (housecoats); these were listed on a second-hand Gestetner duplicating machine, bought in 1938, and copies placed on each table so that customers could read details as they listened to the compère. That Gestetner was kept in repair and not replaced until 1948: such was the drive for economy inherited from the hungry 1930s.

Reginald Howard, at that time buying retail coats, suits and furs, took the lead in organising the fitting of clothing on the models. The most fascinating lesson learnt was how easy it was to pick clothes for some of those who were to show them and how very difficult to find them for others. The conclusion was that what really 'made' a good model was the way she carried herself and the clothes – the measurement that counted was height, which really meant the length of thigh and neck, but carriage was the secret. If buyers were asked 'Why have you given so many garments to Doris White?' the answer was that it was difficult to find things to suit some of the others.

An unusual half-time feature of these parades was a showing of hats by Betty Whelan, whose very attractive face and ability to 'put her head into the hats' (a woman of fashion did not put a hat on her head) sold almost everything she modelled. Betty Whelan developed a successful agency for training models which was equally useful for grooming teenagers.

Finally, pre-war Arnotts decided to resume the recruitment of apprentices, renamed trainees to suggest a fresh start. This practice had fallen into disuse, possibly because of the necessity of reducing staff in the difficult trading of the 1930s, and staff had normally been recruited at 'improver' stage, that is after serving three years as apprentice in another shop, usually a country shop and – if one asked William Nesbitt's opinion – from a shop in one of the 'hardier' northern counties like Cavan. It was hoped that a process of education could produce the stars of the future, or at least a well-trained cadre of managers. In Arnotts' case few of the trainees remained after the age of twenty-five (women had to leave on marriage); those who remained usually became competent and sometimes excellent seniors and managers, but the necessity for securing talent always remained.

A useful source of promising young people was the families of our wholesale customers. As a young man, Victor Hadden, of the Hadden family which owned stores in Carlow, Wexford and Dungarvan, helped to develop Arnotts' training system.

After the war, Arnotts' increasing business recruited up to twenty school leavers as trainees each year. This training in the departments was supplemented by the setting up in Parnell Square Vocational Educational School of three-year day-release courses for trainees in the drapery trade. These courses were supported strongly by the leading department stores and some of the smaller shops until their numbers were thinned out so much by developments in the clothing trade in the 1970s that the leading stores decided it was more economical of valuable time to resume in-house training.

Arnotts also exchanged staff with overseas department stores. Lack of fluency in European languages limited the benefit our young people could derive from this. Students coming to us from Europe were never handicapped by inadequate English.

8 THE EMERGENCY 1939–1945

IN THE SOUTH of Ireland we called the period from 1939 to 1945 'the Emergency', to distance ourselves from the war, in whose outcome we were nevertheless painfully interested. For those who were young at that time, and not fated to die in the conflict, 'It was the best of times, it was the worst of times, it was the spring of hope, it was the winter of despair, we had everything before us, we had nothing before us . . .' to quote again Charles Dickens.

Marooned in our part of the island, precariously cocooned from the war, life became harder and simpler. The scarcity of things encouraged sharing, the dullness of life was enlivened by increased friendships, the contrast with normality was the cause of laughter. Fond memories include cycling miles to a dance at the Zoological Gardens and home afterwards along moonlit roads beautifully free from motor traffic, and sending two lorries with fifty members of staff to help farmers in the Leinster area when bad weather threatened the harvest. That work was considered hard, but the food and drink and fellowship made it memorable.

In the altered circumstances Arnotts adapted as best it could. Annual staff dances, first organised in the 1930s in the old Regal Ballroom in Hawkins Street, continued in the Metropole beside the General Post Office in O'Connell Street. Despite the expense of tickets and, in many cases, suit hire, these 'dress dances' were conducted in style. In 1939, at one of these dances a member of staff (could it have been that excellent workaholic James Rafferty?) assured the author's fiancée, Ella, that the staff were on her side. A rumour had evidently gone round that the match did not meet with maternal approval, which of course lent it romantic appeal. The staff quickly had the opportunity to show their support. The marriage was to take place in September 1939 – during Arnotts' last strike. Ella's dress was stuck half-made in Arnotts' workroom. But the strike picket obligingly moved far enough down Henry Street to allow her to slip into Arnotts and retrieve the dress for Miss Miller, the senior dressmaker, to finish at home in Clontarf.

James Murphy, who started in Arnotts in 1936 as a boy of fourteen, also has a story to tell.

> The staff enjoyed the dance so much that some felt the after-effects more than others. The morning after the dance a young salesman arrived for work inebriated. Superintendent Martin Lawless was horrified but being of a very kind nature said 'Get Rafferty quickly'. Rafferty arrived on the scene with a very large traveller's basket, bundled the helpless young man into it, wheeled him on a trolley across the shop, put him into a van and delivered him safely to his home.

What had been done in Arnotts in the 1930s helped the store to face the Emergency, even if there were doubts about the future. Indeed the year of the phoney war, after the first alarms, may have led to a sense of false security.

Some important trading managers had been appointed before 1940, particularly in the wholesale departments. On the retirement of Patrick Quinn from the underclothing departments in June 1938, Edward McCourt took over. This was a seminal decision. McCourt had been a charge hand in Nicholson Brothers of South William Street. Trained in Belfast, he brought a new efficiency. The blocking of strong competition from Belfast wholesalers by the high import duties of the 1930s had benefited Arnotts' wholesale trade. Horrified to find that knitwear was stored in tea chests on their sides, McCourt set about a thorough reorganisation. He introduced what Arnotts called 'the Belfast system' to ensure by analysis of sales that goods were available to meet the estimated future orders from the six travellers. These were well established in the trade in their own districts which they covered with heavy Bedford vans and a driver; they welcomed McCourt as a breath of fresh air. McCourt used to amuse his staff by saying, 'Let's have the department ship-shape and Protestant-like.'

Other wholesale appointments at the end of 1938 were of Dennis O'Connor as woollen buyer and Michael Hanley as buyer of shirts, including material for the shirt factory. Early in 1939 William McSorley took over and developed the wholesale dress materials and later in the same year Tom Lonergan took charge of the newly created wholesale neckwear department. Finally, and not least importantly, in January 1940 Patrick O'Flaherty, on the death of Francis Hallinan, succeeded him as buyer of the important hosiery department which still included its retail counterparts.

The neckwear department was partly the child of the outfitting buyer's boredom with the retail trade. His name was Dundon and he asked permission to sell wholesale silk shirts, scarves and dressing gowns. He was successful enough, particularly in Dublin, to leave an embryo wholesale department behind him when he resigned. He once offered men's silk shirts to Dermot Tyson of Grafton Street; they were refused but the salesman in the shop said afterwards to Dundon, 'If you had asked him twice the price he would have been impressed enough to take them seriously.'

Looking at the increase of more than 20 per cent in the total of wholesale sales in the year 1939 it is now obvious that the impending war had encouraged Arnotts management to believe that an increase in wholesale trade was possible. Probably, too, William McCormack, a good salesman, was advocating wholesale development, at the time quite correctly.

Between 1939 and 1945 total sales by wholesale increased to £862,000 and by retail to £560,000, in each case by over 2⅓. Over the same period the consumer price index increased by only two-thirds.

But in the retail there was no increase until 1940 when the war sprang into life again, and it was realised rather belatedly that it might be possible for goods to run out almost completely and for the shops to have nothing to sell. At that point it was suggested that our buyer, Dennis

O'Connor, should be authorised to buy £200,000 (about £6 million today) of the most useful worsted material imaginable, say a dark grey flannel suiting. Confronted one afternoon with this rather large idea, which had been designed to shock, William Nesbitt initially said No, but the following morning he returned to the idea, which was discussed and agreed. O'Connor was asked to place the order and reassured that, exceptionally, the goods would not be debited to his department, but would be held in a separate contract account and drawn as required.

Campbell Heather, one of our outstanding wholesale buyers of the following generation, has described Dennis O'Connor as a dignified and much respected man, with an integrity and code of behaviour of a very high standard; that standard, declared Campbell Heather, was shared by almost all of Arnotts' buyers. O'Connor was tall and impressive in appearance, and he was, like Arnotts' leading buyers, completely trusted by the managing director; as the war progressed and supplies became scarce, O'Connor and other buyers often left Arnotts on a Monday morning with £10,000 in their pockets; Arnotts always aimed to pay promptly, but then cash was king.

That purchase of grey worsted flannel was an appalling risk in the political and military circumstances; it involved putting up half the money in advance to a stranger in Sweden who bought the wool in South Africa and had it spun and woven into cloth in Northern Italy. Only £100,000 worth was secured in the end, but that was an outstanding success. It helped to nourish the tailoring workroom to a size which, in 1945, required the building of a second new floor to the Prince's Street workroom.

Sewing thread, another basic necessity of the drapery trade, was also in threatened shortage. Willie Cummins recalled that Arnotts was fortunate to secure quantities of Coats black and white reels from Northern Ireland which were delivered in large sacks.

If Arnotts' buyers could not get goods in short supply for money alone, they tried to get it by charm instead; for example, Paddy O'Flaherty, hosiery buyer, always acted the stage Irishman on his trips to Britain. On one occasion a directors' meeting of a well known hosiery manufacturer had to be adjourned while O'Flaherty gave the directors an exhibition of hurling. Paddy had won an All Ireland medal with the Dubs. The O'Flahertys were a notable Arnotts family. Paddy had married 'from stock' and both his father and his son, Patrick, worked in Arnotts; even his grandson, Gerard, was a trainee in Boyers.

Sometimes buyers had to earn the admiration of their suppliers, a feat accomplished by Dennis O'Connor. When invited by Italian woollen manufacturers to have a drink from a well-stocked drinks cabinet, he said, 'Start on the right' and worked from there across the cabinet towards the left until his hosts capitulated.

Arnotts' good relations with Irish woollen and linen manufacturers were of immense value during this period of shortages. Foxford tweed was a basic material and Flynn's of Sixmilebridge produced blanket material that found its way into many tight corners. Arnotts thanked God and the government's economic nationalism of the 1930s for the development of new knitting and making-up industries which became vital during the period of the Emergency and were very useful for years afterwards.

This access to manufacturing sources achieved by Arnotts' wholesale buying was of great help to the garment workrooms and therefore to the retail garment buyers. Arnotts was always open to buy, urging managers to buy from any suitable source, even from competitors, once to their great surprise from Todd Burns in Mary Street who also ran workrooms though they were not so broadminded.

In 1939 the retirement of Miss Coyne opened the way for the appointment of more women buyers. Miss Braiden, who had been appointed to Inex in 1937, took over Miss Coyne's frocks while Doris Cooney and Mary Farrelly took her lingerie department, split into lingerie and children's respectively. These two were exceptionally successful buyers. Taking over a total trade of about £6,000 a year in each case, by 1945 they had brought it up to £29,000 for lingerie and £38,000 for children's, that is five and six times compared with the average in Arnotts of two and one-third times.

Doris Cooney, who was tall, dark haired and reserved in manner, split her department into two, lingerie and corsets, so that the sales staff in the latter could be trained to specialise in fitting; she had exquisite taste and sold the most beautiful lingerie and housecoats at the height of the post-war boom.

Unfortunately for Arnotts, at that high point Doris Cooney opted for marriage; her happiness was wished more ruefully than was usual at that time. Mary Farrelly was bright and bustling, and also reached a peak in trade post-war; having established a firm base for later development of our children's trade up to school-leaving age she, too, married – again a great loss to Arnotts.

One other woman appointed as buyer in 1941 must be mentioned. Her name was Winifred Gorry. She was a sales assistant in Clerys when she called one day to ask the manager if she could start a department selling felt material. William Nesbitt asked what were its uses, to be told it was used for making things. He was very impressed with her quiet, politely confident manner and asked her to start work in one month, on giving due notice. After leaving the room, she knocked again on the door, which was always left open except during meetings and confidential interviews, put her head round it and asked if he would order felt material now, so she would have it to work with when she started. She surprised him by sending in an order for £600 worth, or the best part of £20,000 in today's money. He ordered half the quantity and felt a bit small when after a month of selling she came to ask for more. Winifred Gorry was a modest but extremely clever buyer with outstanding taste. Her first department was called 'Notions'; in wartime she resorted to selling semi-antique jewellery. She will reappear later in this story.

In an effort to find new ranges of goods under the import duties of the 1930s and the war scarcities of the early 1940s, Arnotts used branding extensively and registered all trade names. The law required that names could not be 'descriptive of the nature or quality of the goods' so it was often difficult or impossible to secure registration. The shirt factory once started to use the name 'Dri-Fab' for shirts made of quick-drying material and only then urged the registration of the name. This was, of course, refused. But since the names of the cutter and the manager of the factory were Farrell and Bonner, Dri-Fab (Farrell and Bonner) was allowed on appeal. An unexpected away win.

Other arguments with government occurred after Allied forces were driven from France in 1940 and the Irish government hastened to force the clothing trade to take action to minimise the war's effect by rationing and price control.

Rationing of food was accepted by nearly everyone as reasonable, and, with control of some prices, helped to keep the household budget down at a time when young married couples might allow only £2 a week for it.

Rationing of clothing was not considered reasonable by the drapery trade. It was known that quite a large section of the population depended on second-hand clothes and this was confirmed later by the ready sale for £1 each of the clothing coupons from the ration books of those who had no use for them.

The unions involved in the drapery trade urged the employers in the Drapers' Chamber of Trade to join in protest against clothes rationing. Arnotts had joined the chamber in 1934 and so found itself represented at a meeting in 1942 which decided almost unanimously on a protest march; the only ones to vote against were the author and Ruairí Brugha. We believed marching was hardly likely to wring the hearts of a public struggling with shortages of white bread, tea, fuel, sugar and other imported goods.

The march was one of the most embarrassing events in the author's life. Placed, because of Arnotts' prominence in the trade and despite his renewed protests, in the front row between Edward McGuire of Brown Thomas and Denis Guiney of Clerys, he felt dwarfed by the elegant stature of the former and the more bulky dominance of the latter. Fortunately, it was a fine day; the walk in procession formed on Parnell Square and ended at Leinster House attracting only moderate interest and no reaction, hostile or jocular.

The drapery trade also protested every time the margins were 'controlled' by government order. Before the war margins of 33⅓ per cent on selling price were common for goods sold by retail and of 20 per cent on selling for those sold wholesale; in steps these were reduced for clothing to 25 per cent for retail and 15 per cent for wholesale. This turned out to be good for the drapery trade because it made less desirable goods more attractive to the customers in conditions of shortage, and prices were rising anyway. Most importantly wages were controlled by the Standstill Order of May 1941.

An annoying decision by the Department of Industry and Commerce affected the making up trade – in Arnotts' case this included the dress factory Milne Models. In addition to rationing, the UK had introduced control of styles for women's outerwear to save materials – shorter lengths of skirts, few pleats, and plain cut generally. The women's clothing group in the Federation of Irish Manufacturers suggested to the department that the use of materials be controlled by specifying a maximum yardage for each size and type of garment – jackets, skirt, dress – leaving designers free in the important matter of style. The department accepted control of materials and also imposed the UK restrictions on style. At least one manufacturer of women's clothing vowed never to offer free advice to a government department again.

The Emergency was not the most cheerful of times and this seemed to show itself in the heightened importance of pastoral letters, lenten regulations and above all the activities of the self-appointed guardians of public morals. Complaints about unseemly displays of women's underwear, particularly corsets, in Arnotts' windows, were always made by the self-appointed: 'The Archbishop's secretary will be very upset to hear of this' they would say. On the other hand, a Co. Wexford priest wrote praising an advertisement using a photograph of a girl wearing a spotted summer dress. He called her the best type of Irish woman. Arnotts never had condemnation from the clergy.

Newspapers naturally showed regard for the opinions of their readers. The *Irish Independent* insisted that Arnotts cut off the legs of any figure of a woman wearing a corset in an advertisement; this added considerably to costs of production since the other morning and evening Dublin newspapers were able to accept legs.[1]

In June 1936 the Merchant Drapers had agreed with the Distributive Workers' Union on a new minimum scale of wages which was still in force at the beginning of the Emergency. This was modified in June 1940 by a cost of living bonus for staff with ten years' service of 6s 6d for men and 4s 6d for women. In 1941 the Merchant Drapers' Association was liquidated; Arnotts had been refused any compensation for costs of closure during the Ronayne strike, but received a cheque for £429 from the assets on liquidation. Complying with the Trade Union Act of 1941, Arnotts joined the new Federated Union of Employers. The Dublin drapery branch negotiated minimum wages and conditions from then onwards.

Table 8.1: Minimum rates for retail distributive staff, 1936

Year	Men	Women	Typists, Cashiers
1	15s	15s	20s
2	20s	20s	25s
3	30s	25s	30s
4	40s	35s	40s
5	50s	42s 6d	45s
6/7	60s	50s	50s
8	72s 6d	62s 6d	50s

[1] A little story may illustrate a seachange in public sensitivities in the still under-age Irish State. In 1918 a boy of five was given a little pair of trunks to wear when going for a bathe before breakfast with his father beside the Martello Tower at Seapoint, Co. Dublin; the boy, now long an adult, remembers vividly the laughter of all the men who were bathing in their birthday suits. In 1939, as a recently married man, he came to live in the same district and went down to bathe before breakfast without any trunks. He had just left the water, and had a towel around him, when a girl came down to bathe. 'That was a close shave', he said to a man towelling beside him, who replied, 'Yes, I thought you were cutting it fine. A fellow was had up for indecent exposure here a few weeks ago. A man in one of those houses over there saw him with binoculars and reported him to the police.'

From these retail rates Arnotts deducted shillings from the fourth year onwards to be 'earned up' by commission on sales made. In the eighth year this deduction was 12s 6d for men and 10s for women.

It happened only very rarely in Arnotts that commission was so low that the minimum rate in a six-month period had to be made up – in most cases commission earned for staff substantially more than the minimum rate.

Transport workers were paid slightly less and started work younger than salespeople; James Murphy gives his account of the busy morning's work of a boy in Arnotts.

> The wage was 14 shillings for a 48-hour week. Every Monday morning at 8 a.m. the stonework of the display windows in Henry Street had to be cleaned with whitening. After cleaning the windows he then went into the shop to vacuum the carpets and dust the showcases. He then collected the parcels for delivery from the salespeople before 10.30 a.m. These would be brought by the same boys to the parcel office for sorting which would take 30 minutes approximately; these parcels had to be ready for delivery at 11 a.m. The junior boys did the city deliveries on bicycles and the senior boys went in the vans to the suburbs. All these boys were responsible for collecting cash and they would give receipts for the money. Any shortage had to be made good by the boy.
>
> The senior boys had to sweep the wholesale departments and each boy was responsible for his own brush which had his own number on it. Wet sawdust was prepared in buckets the evening before for the sweeping. After sweeping, the senior boys would carry the ledgers from the strong-room for the clerks. They then attended to their deliveries.
>
> These boys had a great sense of humour and were full of life. On one occasion a boy, Tommy Creighton, caught a mouse and put it into one of the Lamson tube carriers and ran down to the cash office to see the effect. Imagine the uproar among the ladies when the carrier was opened!

At the top table at the centenary dinner 1943 in the original basement cafe were (from left): William McCormack, Ella Nesbitt, James Fagan (Senior), Fortescue Monsell, Mrs Fagan, William Nesbitt, J. Healy, Mrs Nesbitt, Patrick O'Connor (partially obscured), Margaret Kerrigan (being served)

Golf Society outing September 1944

Wages were controlled during and after the war but by 1948 various 'Emergency' bonuses had been added under standard rate orders of the Department of Industry and Commerce, which increased the 1939 rates by 63–72 per cent compared with the rise in the consumer price index of about 78 per cent. It was remarkable that in those war years the consumer price index came by degrees to be accepted by both parties to those interminable meetings in the smoke-filled rooms of the Federated Union of Employers. Before that, trade union secretaries had to rely on wordy generalisations about the effect of rising costs on their members' standard of living, as most of those present in desperation lit yet another cigarette.

With wage costs rising by about three-quarters and sales by two and one-third times during the period 1939–45 alone, it is not surprising that overall costs in Arnotts dropped from the pre-war rate of 13½ per cent on sales to little more than 10 per cent, allowing net profit to rise to double the pre-war £14,000. Stocks rose dramatically to peak in 1943 at three times the pre-war level bringing money turn down to four times. Naturally, the value of stocks caused some doubts and an undeclared reserve, accepted by the auditors, and tax paid, was held against it. Dividends, of course, were controlled and continued at the pre-war 7½ per cent on the ordinary capital throughout.

Arnotts' centenary in 1943 was celebrated modestly with an illuminated address from the staff to the directors containing a list of the names of 181 men and 107 women of the distributive staff. A large dinner party was held in Arnotts' café for staff and two separate dances were organised by the social committees of the members of the Distributive and the Transport Unions. The highlights of the dinner party were a speech by Hugh Neary, the senior buyer, proposing the health of the company and a hilarious account by Paddy Murphy, transport manager, of the adventures of the gas-driven delivery vans with their high rectangular white canvas balloons on top; on some occasions he wondered if the vans would ever return!

The period of the Emergency brought a doubling of the retail cash trade compared with retail credit sales; before

1939 the two had been very evenly balanced for years. With the developing trade of Henry Street after the Second World War cash has remained the larger element in Arnotts' retail trade. The rate of stock turn, however, dropped by half because goods were available despite forebodings. Carrying these relatively larger stocks and debtors forced an increase in bank borrowing – this required a change in the articles to increase the authorised figure to £500,000.

Arnotts' gift token, copied from the book token idea (launched in 1932) and first issued in 1939, was very convenient at a time when the range of goods was limited and erratic. Sales of gift tokens grew slowly to a figure of perhaps £10,000 a year by the end of the Emergency. The token was originally intended for Christmas giving but was soon redesigned to be valid all year; later, special cards were issued for wedding gifts, and sales of tokens have grown in recent years to over £1 million.

Arnotts' Sales in July and January were called 'Emergency Sales' to stress that they could not be expected to stand comparison with normal Sales, and by July 1941 they had been shortened to three weeks. In practice, a Sale lasting for a month had proved to be very busy for two weeks, with a normal level of trading in the third week and a flurry of final clearances in the last week. This wartime experience of shorter Sales led from 1950 onwards to a policy of running Sales for only two and a half weeks with large reductions in prices right from the start. The half-year's trading could then be closed on 15 July and 15 January and new goods opened for display while possible competitors were still labouring to sell the old.

Further extension of the site also proved possible during those years. For some time Arnotts had been attempting to secure possession of the shops fronting on Henry Street in numbers 7 and 8, which were let to tenants and in one case condemned by Dublin Corporation. The arrival of James Fagan on the board started a series of attempts to gain possession by legal process. These failed; in the case of the condemned building a grant of a new 21-year lease was awarded by the court. Persuasion by William Nesbitt succeeded where legal process failed and these leases were bought out. In 1945 Arnotts also broke through to Middle Abbey Street, realising that numbers 102, 103 and 104 matched exactly the width of the workroom buildings between Prince's Street and Abbey Street and finding the freehold of these three shops for sale.

The Emergency, too, saw the setting up of Arnotts' staff pension fund, agreed by the directors in 1938. This considerable, and possibly open-ended, expense required courage not only on the part of the directors but also on the part of the staff, who authorised Jack Young and Harry Healy to negotiate on their behalf. It is difficult now to realise how forward-looking a step this was. Many companies over the next twenty years found themselves in serious trouble over unfunded staff pension schemes.

Pension aims were a minimum of £2 for men and 30 shillings a week for women after forty years service on the basic scale given in Table 8.1 (page 116). Graded contributions of equal size from the company and the member were agreed up to a basic salary limit of £750 a year. This scheme was set up by the Sun Life Company of Canada. Trustees were to be appointed by the directors of the company, three to be chosen by the directors and two nominated by the members. Jack Young argued strongly for an equal number of trustees but the directors cautiously felt safer with a majority. For years, Young was the right-hand man of company secretaries from Monsell to O'Sullivan: a man for detail and hard work in the best Arnotts tradition.

Membership of the staff pension fund was optional for those already working in Arnotts, subject to an upper age limit, and the older members joining had pensions for past service paid up at half-rate by the company. Only one or two of the sales staff did not join. The fund had been agreed with representatives of the Irish Union of Distributive Workers and not with the members of the second largest union working in Arnotts, the Irish Transport and General Workers Union. At that time, the negotiation of one scheme to cover both unions would have been very difficult, involving, for the women at least, very different attitudes and rates of pay.

For the latter in 1944, a similar contributory scheme with slightly lower benefits, administered by Arnotts, was registered as a friendly society under the name Alexander Pension Fund – a tribute to the late Alexander Nesbitt. In this Conor O'Brien, the highly respected union representative working in Arnotts' transport department, played a leading part, with Thomas Noone and David Woodlock. Earlier in that year, these three had rented rooms, on behalf of Arnotts' employees' club, on the second floor over H. Williams's building in Henry Street to house a billiards table; the rent of £165 a year was guaranteed by the directors of Arnotts. These moves delighted the members of the Irish Transport Union working in the store.[2] The directors made yearly payments into the Alexander Fund of £1,500, the sixth and final one in 1953.

Unfortunately, there was a high rate of withdrawal among the women members of the Alexander Fund and a tendency among the younger men to wish for a non-contributory fund. The resignation of Conor O'Brien as trustee of the fund, on his appointment to office in the ITGWU, did not help. In 1957 the members voted in general meeting for closure of the fund and Arnotts' directors assumed responsibility for paying pensions earned to that date.

In later years, membership of Arnotts' staff pension fund was offered to skilled craftsmen and more highly paid members of unions other than the Distributive Workers, and with fewer members employed in unions other than IDATU, membership of Arnotts' staff fund is now a condition of all permanent (including part-time) employment. Alexander Nesbitt would have been very satisfied with this democratic outcome.

---

[2]They had presented a handsome barometer as a 100th birthday present to the directors; it was hung just inside the store on one of the massive piers holding up the tower.

9 AFTERGLOW 1945–1948

THE ENDING OF the war in Europe in May 1945 brought an outbreak of euphoria, not only in the United Kingdom, but also in the Republic of Ireland. It was not the end of the Emergency, which historians prefer to date to about 1948 – it takes time to dismantle an apparatus of central government control. For Arnotts, until a set-back in 1952 linked with the Korean War, it was a time of rapidly increasing trade.

Total sales in 1944, the last full year of war, were slightly less than the year before at £1.192 million. In calendar year 1945 they jumped to £1.458 million and peaked at £2.506 million in 1947 (and again in 1951 at £2.704 million). Stocks at the end of 1944 had dropped to £164,000 at cost but were built up rapidly from 1946 to 1948 to a new peak of £510,000; by the end of 1949 they were back to £275,000.

Numerous visitors from England and elsewhere came to buy clothing, two suits to measure at a time, or the most expensive and beautiful housecoats and lingerie. Others came for food, a good fillet steak or real pork sausages; eyes widened at the sight of legs of lamb, until their price caused the buyer, accustomed to a meat ration at a controlled price, to halt in his or her tracks.

By 1945, Arnotts had finally set up separate accounts for all retail and wholesale departments. By allocating overheads rather roughly, and perhaps unfairly, according to sales, one could estimate a net profit for each. Clearly, this was a great step forward in control of those often over-mighty barons, the buyers. The number of departments had increased, to fifteen wholesale and twenty-six retail, mostly by the separation of the two sides of the trade; but McCourt had started a new department in wholesale (ladieswear) for women's knitwear and blouses, O'Flaherty another (hand-wear) for gloves and O'Riordan, coming to us from Cork, had replaced Leahy as buyer of trimmings (wholesale) and haberdashery (retail).

In retail, after some Nesbitt agonising over the morality of the thing, a department was born for cosmetics, which was later adopted fully into the family and rechristened 'beauty shop'. The idea of the beauty shop was suggested to Arnotts by director Patrick O'Connor, who declared Switzers was doing very well in what proved to be a rapidly developing business, one which seems to thrive even in bad times.

In retail, furniture sales were double pre-war levels under a new buyer, Samuel Scott. Carpets and soft furnishings, starved of goods, had not been able to increase despite the appointment of George Crampton. Linens under Hugh Neary had also doubled. Silks under another new buyer, Samuel Dillon, was three and a half times pre-war levels.[1] Dillon, however, ran into trouble as soon as he was able to over-buy printed rayon material from Switzerland after the war; the import quota available was quite inadequate to cope with his orders and much had to be returned to our great embarrassment. Some of our buyers of other departments ran into the wake of Dillon's over-large orders when they were buying later from the same manufacturers.

Two outstanding retail buyers who have not yet been mentioned were Jack Connor with his shoe department and Margaret Kerrigan, buyer of scarves, handkerchiefs and lace in a department called 'novelties'. Jack Connor was a kindly and deeply religious non-conformist who attended services at Merrion Hall. His shoe department developed successfully during the war and after, and laid the foundations for our outstanding success in shoes after

---

[1] Pre-war, the silk buyer is remembered as spending most of his time in a stock space behind his department cutting up 'remnants' for the next Sale. During the 1930s a number of retail departments had become far too dependent on the Sales.

1950. Margaret Kerrigan, who had started buying in 1934, was always successful in her smaller department and always reliable; she developed an air of authority to suit the position of her department in the centre front of the store.

In 1946 a new retail department was created by separating women's knitted outerwear from the hosiery department and combining it with women's blouses and skirts – it was eventually called 'separates'. The first buyer recruited was the lively, plump, rather overwhelming saleswoman, Dolly O'Hare, who founded a department for which we have always remembered her. Alec Nesbitt, who manufactured the Highland brand knitwear, complained that too many 'specials', that is, orders for just one garment, were being procured by telephone from a stock held in the factory. He suggested a plan for stock-holding which entailed scaling orders so that three dozen of the most popular colour, 'prairie rose', would be ordered but only a single garment in the least popular colour, yellow. In fact the department had no idea of the extent to which they were under-ordering what was most in demand. One of the senior assistants was given charge of the stock and of filling the plan; in fear and trembling Stasia Kavanagh undertook the task and in no time at all sales were doubled as a result of the availability of the stocks most in demand. Stasia courageously invested a legacy from her mother in Arnotts ordinary £4 shares before they were split into £1 and increased in number by the bonus issue of two for one in 1957; five years later she saw her holding double again. Buyers in Arnotts usually invested in shares but, until later rights issues to staff, there were relatively few shareholders among the rank and file.

By 1946, John O'Reilly had developed the man's shop into the largest single retail department (the two women's departments for outerwear combining coats, suits and dresses, added together, were larger). O'Reilly rode this period of difficult post-war trading with unusual skill. He explained that in the immediate post-war boom he wrote out his usual orders and then forced himself to double them, because he knew he could sell much more than usual; when the trough in trading replaced the boom he

During the 1940s, many city firms organised groups to help with the harvest. Arnott's harvest army in 1946 included Charlie Dunne (top left) and Cecil McGovern (second from right, standing)

had to do the reverse by halving his normal orders – a more difficult operation. This statement by O'Reilly was positively Socratic in its self-knowledge. After an outstanding career of great service to Arnotts he died tragically on the eve of his retirement, leaving an extravagant hidden reserve of profit in his stock. He had once produced a figure at stock-taking which was some thousands short of the control figure; he took this shortage badly and in two days time had 'found' the difference.

From time to time Arnotts' auditors, Craig Gardner, worried about the lack of a 'marking-off' room, that is a separate office for matching goods delivered with the invoices which were presented for payment. Management preferred to trust the buyer-managers; after all, with so many different types and sizes of goods, who were the most interested in seeing to their safe arrival? In fact occasional rows broke out when a badly written department number steered goods into the wrong department, and a buyer absent at markets, who had not briefed his assistant department manager, allowed goods to lie unavailable to the rightful owners.

Arnotts' organisation is efficient for its purpose because it is very flat in shape. The relationship between the managing director and the buyers reminds one of the mediaeval feudal system, but that system served well in simpler, less organised times and successful trading must remain adaptable; at least Arnotts has reached the Magna Carta stage of having a defined code of conduct between Crown and Barons.

Essentially there are three levels in Arnotts' organisation. In trading there are the managing directors, the buyers/assistant department managers (ADMs), and the sales assistants; and in the offices the company secretary, the office managers/ADMs and the clerks. Success depends not only on the ability of each, but also very much on good relationships. Genius is not expected and Arnotts is particularly uncomfortable with a prima donna. A trainee is really a beginner only three ranks from the top. Truly, there can be a marshal's baton in every private's knapsack.

A challenge to management's faith in the buyers surfaced at least twice among the directors in this post-war decade. The view was that a merchandise manager was needed; as if such an all-wise saviour, interposed as an additional layer of management, would ensure salvation!

In trading, the scene is expected to change continually and the value of members of staff lies not in what they are or know at the moment, but in what they can learn or become. If a genius of a merchandise manager is found to fill the imagined role he or she should be appointed managing director of trading.

A weakness at times has been the relationship between the department manager (buyer) and the assistant department manager (ADM); the latter should be encouraged to graduate to buying manager by delegation of limited authority such as 'filling in' on established lines for a start, and standing in completely for the department manager eventually. Very useful relationships can be developed between an experienced manager and a younger ADM with new trading ideas or flair, who still needs to learn trading wisdom. It is essential both that the senior manager be confident enough of his or her own secure position to teach the junior by passing on knowledge and experience, revealing hesitations and doubts as well as hopes and plans, and that the junior should respect and admire the senior. Certainly, some compatibility of temperament is needed too.

The managing director responsible for overview of a number of trading departments should be concerned about the pattern of relationships in the departments under his or her control. These will develop and alter, and only by working closely with staff can the manager hope to be really directing.

William Nesbitt was, beneath his cloak of righteousness, a soft-hearted man and a democrat; he showed more interest in the skilled craftsman than the middle-class salesman. Above all, he brought to managing direction an acute sense of humour. He loved the occasional malapropisms produced by Arnotts staff.

'Where is Mr Lawless?'

'He is downstairs in contemplation with Mr Murphy.'

This suggested only too well a leisurely pace of business. William did realise that it was difficult to account for some behaviour, even in the best of people. One of his favourite quotations was a rather free translation of Martial's epigram, 'I do not love you, Dr Fell, the reason why I cannot tell.' Human nature, he concluded, did not lend itself to the simplification he so loved. He was also able to join in the fun, as James Murphy relates. 'When Mr Chambers, buyer of the wholesale shoes, damaged the firm's car and went to Paddy Murphy transport manager, to have the matter sorted out, Paddy told Mr Chambers to "Go to hell". Whereupon Mr Chambers went to Mr William to complain saying, "Mr Murphy told me to go to Hell". Mr William said: "Why come to me? Do you think I'm the Devil ?"'

To cope with the work of giving change in our increasing cash trade we installed after the war a new Lamson pneumatic tube cash system. This was inadequate. In busy departments at lunchtime peaks the delivery of change was at times so slow that the senior superintendent, Martin Lawless, would run downstairs to find out what had happened to it, or, in desperation and somewhat to the surprise of the customer, give change out of his own pocket. Within about fifteen years most of the retail departments on the ground floor had cash registers.

It is difficult to recapture the agony of inadequate systems of change-giving at busy times in department stores. During Christmas 1963, Michael Nesbitt was a trainee in Selfridges in London's Oxford Street selling, with another young Irishman, an adaptable basket of gold coloured wire for 9s 11d; this was so popular that having enough pennies to give in change became a desperate problem for which only a desperate solution was possible. It took so long to get pennies, and management was so unable to solve the problem, that Michael's companion broke all rules, took £1 out of the till (rule one), ran out by the main doors in Oxford Street (rule two), boarded the next bus, got 240 pence from the very willing conductor for Selfridge's £1 and ran back to his department.

Working in the store in the post-war years (above) fancy goods
(below) packing shirts

Arnotts' first two cash registers were sold by National Cash Registers' salesman, Knill. NCR believed that a separate drawer was necessary for each sales assistant. They were not very neat pieces of machinery in any case but with, say, six drawers underneath for six sales staff they bulked very large. In the 1940s, one transaction in five arose in the haberdashery department. During the Sales, many items sold at one penny, and the illegibly scribbling assistants and understandably careless customers covered the floor with the sales dockets which 'for security' were written with duplicate for every transaction. So the haberdashery department, which was in two sections, got two NCR registers. This, of course, did away with the writing of sales bills because they printed dockets as receipts as well as recording totals of sales. Obviously the sales analysis done by registers suggested their extension to other departments, but this was delayed by Knill's abandonment of NCR in favour of Sweda registers. Sweda held the contrary belief that only one cash drawer was required since this encouraged staff to make sure that their fellows did not abuse the system. It took Arnotts' management a year or so to swallow the new doctrine.

The war and its afterglow had done Arnotts' balance sheet no harm. Premises, which in 1945 had actually been written down to £25,000 (the trough of achievement), had by January 1949 crept up again to £42,000, which was still £7,000 short of the January 1940 figure. Profit after tax had risen to £40,000 (1940: £15,000), balance forward to next account £80,000 (1940: £6,000) and dividends had risen from the wartime level of 7½ per cent to 11¼ per cent.

Fortunately no one in Dublin seemed to have learned the word 'takeover'. The author, who had been co-opted a director in 1948, did suggest a 'merger' with Switzers, with whose directors relations were good, to be told bluntly by his father, 'You can't manage this place. Why do you think you could manage Switzers ?'

Architect Ian Roberts reminds us that in 1949, the impressive 56 foot high copperdomed tower, and the flanking towers at either end, were removed (inset shows how it looked). They badly needed repair and 'served no useful purpose', said Arnotts' chairman. Perhaps the new 1993 glass-domed atrium makes some amends.

10 BUILD-UP IN HENRY STREET 1948–1960

THE REBUILDING OF numbers 7 to 10 Henry Street had been decided on in 1945 but it was 1955 by the time the steel girders were ordered. In the meantime, in 1954, a roof level was added to the workroom building between Prince's Street and Abbey Street, and its central well was filled in to complete the first and second floors below. That second floor, later linked to the roof level in Henry Street, is now Arnotts' exhibition hall.

In December 1958 a contract for the rebuilding was signed with J. & D. McIlvena. The architect was Geoffrey Henry of Donnelly and Henry. His design, with an elegant solution to the problem of achieving wide spacing of pillars, extended the basement, ground and balcony levels of the 1898 building and linked in L shape with the first, second and top floors along Henry Street. The new curtain wall in blue, green and terracotta panels on Henry Street was a design of the time, but many may now regret that the Victorian facade of 11 to 15 Henry Street was not extended. Pastiche, however, can easily become ridiculous, as can be seen elsewhere in Dublin.

William Nesbitt agreed to spend £100,000 on three levels of this building; later he accepted the six levels as designed. The total cost, including fees, was £250,000. Meanwhile, retail and wholesale departments and factory workrooms had been developed; the idea was to keep everything conveniently in the Henry Street/Abbey Street area.

There was a final post-war peak in wholesale trade in 1950 and 1951, but a sharp drop in sales of as much as a quarter in 1952 to £1.286 million came with the Korean War. Recovery was slow; total sales in 1960 barely reached the high point of 1951. In that period the consumer price index rose from 348 to 466, most noticeably during the Korean War; this movement of prices was reflected more clearly in retail sales.

Part of the explanation for this poor wholesale performance was a change in the nature of Arnotts' trade from cloth to clothing. Despite the appointment of Jim Hughes to buyer of wholesale and retail cotton piece goods, a job he did so exceptionally well that he was the obvious choice as wholesale manager in 1958, there was, overall, a notable decline in the piece-goods trade. The gap was closed by a strong performance in women's coats and hats bought by Thomas Kinsley, one of Arnotts' trainees, and John Collier. But, in total, a larger increase came from the three departments of Eddie McCourt; on his early retirement in 1952 his mantle fell on Campbell Heather.

Campbell Heather had started as an apprentice in 1937 in Nicholson Brothers of South William Street under McCourt. In 1940, when his time was finished, he took the train to Belfast and joined the Irish Guards. In 1942 he was commissioned in the 2nd Punjab Regiment, Indian Army, and was discharged in April 1946 having been wounded in Burma.[1] He returned to Nicholsons but McCourt soon asked him to join him in Arnotts.

In 1950 Heather took over the buying of a department called 'rayons' for the new 'artificial' dress materials; he succeeded his friend, Joseph Monan. In 1952 he succeeded Eddie McCourt in the children's department. In the late 1950s, Heather rapidly developed this trade creating a new department, junior coats, in 1958, of which his ADM Ross Dallas soon took over the buying, and another department,

---

[1] In his retirement Campbell Heather was made an honorary MBE for his work as secretary to the committee which restored to its intended splendour the Irish National War Memorial at Islandbridge for Irishmen killed in the two world wars, designed by Sir Edwin Lutyens. This is now a worthy memorial lying along a ridge over that pleasant open stretch of the River Liffey, about three miles from the centre of Dublin, used by the rowing clubs. Access for cars is along the road leading to the Trinity College boathouse.

babywear, in 1961 which he ran with his original children's department until his retirement in 1980.

This was an extraordinary creation of trade, each of these departments becoming relatively large in size. Part of the secret was Heather's willingness to offer to another the management of what he had developed, which showed a most unusual generosity of spirit. He was one of a number of wholesale buyers who traded up in the wholesale division and showed that a fruitful partnership with his retail counterpart could be expected. In the 1930s management had separated the two streams for greater understanding and control. Now the problem was to encourage the two to work together, the wholesaler supplying the greater buying strength and the retailer the drive to improve quality and styling.

A quasi-collegiate relationship between wholesale and retail buyers was also achieved by Thomas Lonergan, (member of an Irish hockey team which won the Triple Crown), who developed the new wholesale neckwear department. The high import duties on made-up goods in the 1950s encouraged heavy buying of scarves, squares and handkerchief in the piece. Margaret Kerrigan, the retail buyer, travelled regularly to France, Switzerland and Northern Italy with Lonergan and this tradition was carried on by Mary Tallon, her ADM and successor.

It was not always easy to reconcile the taste of the retail trade with the quantities required in the wholesale. William Nesbitt believed that Arnotts' friendly rival, Switzers, bought from London wholesalers or agents who had, before Arnotts, picked over the French, Swiss or Italian ranges and presumably, like John West, taken the best. In the hope that they had not, Arnotts valued the keener prices which came by larger buying from the manufacturers, especially as these quantities would be suitable for the final hemming or fringing operations carried out in an Irish factory to save import duty. Lonergan regularly sold large quantities to the Irish buyer of Woolworths, also based in Henry Street, for their chain of shops in the Republic.

The period of high import duties and quotas which began in 1932 and lasted until the Anglo-Irish Free Trade

Agreement's reduction of them over the years 1965–75, and especially during the Second World War, made it imperative for Arnotts' buyers to encourage Irish manufacturing.

Arnotts' own factories and workrooms also made their contribution to local production. At one stage, William Nesbitt was ready to start a new sewing operation wherever he could find vacant rooms. He was particularly keen on women's hats, always hoping for their return to centre stage in the world of fashion, but he would support with great enthusiasm any proposal for manufacturing.

Our largest true factory, in the sense that it developed a trade with the whole of Ireland and at one time exported 60 per cent of its production, was what is today called Ballet International, which manufactured women's underwear. This was the creation of Mrs Joan Lawler, an exceptionally capable member of yet another 'Arnotts family'; her two sisters also played parts in our retail success, Mary (Kerr) in our corset department and Nell (Murphy) in our separates.

Joan Lawler started in Arnotts in 1942 as a trainee, was seconded to Sam Scott, furniture buyer, to help with his office work, then briefly, after the end of clothes rationing, cleared the glorious confusion of Arnotts' coupons and from there moved to keeping the accounts of some of the sewing workrooms.

Under her management, with the financial backing and approval of Arnotts' directors, Ballet Foundations established itself as very profitable, generating in most years, after full corporation tax, a cash flow more than sufficient to cover all but the largest capital expenditure. The story of Ballet proves that it was possible for Arnotts to initiate a successful manufacturing subsidiary. It was hoped the shirt factory would follow the same route, and Joan Lawler was asked to undertake its direction. Perhaps she was wise to refuse to enter a trade that has largely gone East! Her own process called for very detailed and skilled machining in which European factories can still hope to hold their own.

Joan Lawler was a strong manager in that she brought decisions to the directors rather than problems. She earned the Veuve Clicquot accolade as Business Woman of the Year, was a director of Arnotts from 1985 until her retirement in 1988 and is now passing on to others her acquired skills in the Industrial Development Authority's Mentor Programme. Her account of the Ballet story appears in Chapter 11.

The Milne Models dress factory had a good post-war period despite the departure of the energetic Margaret Forkan, who refused to admit that some of the precious materials she had stored for some years on her shelves were past their sell-by date. Selling was in the hands of Nathaniel McNabb who kept things going through a period of changing factory managers. At first he drove a small Ford 8 cwt van which had been altered to carry sample dresses hanging full length on rails, except for long evening dresses which had to be looped up on their hangers; this entailed raising the roof of the van by about eighteen inches. It was rudely nicknamed the top hat, and was once overturned by the wind on one of the many bends of the road between Galway and Clifden; McNabb just reported the incident without comment.

The success of Milne Models and a size chart for women's dresses in an American trade magazine suggested further specialisation in the dress trade. The sizing called 'Miss' in American fittings rose in two inch hip fittings; for example 36", 38", 40" were the usual sizes but they did go up to 50". This seemed more accurate than the pre-war London SW (small woman), W (woman), WX (larger woman), OS (outsize), XOS (extra outsize). A very large washing woman once asked Agnes Nesbitt (William's wife) to buy her a pair of the splendid Swiss 'Comfort' knickers, saying, 'I dunno the size, mam – how about XSOS?'

The corresponding bust fittings in Miss sizing were two inches less than the hip sizes, that is 34", 36", 38" and so on, and the waist sizes ten inches less at 26", 28", 30". These were the 'ideal' slim young woman's measurements. Since teenage girls were often smaller-waisted but temporarily fuller-figured elsewhere, and many older women, who had borne children, fuller in the waist and relatively shorter in length for their size, in 1944 Arnotts opened a new

Arnotts always combined manufacturing with retailing: Harry Carrick
demonstrating how Arnotts' 'Everest' mattresses were made

John Doody (second from right) and three buyers, (from left) John
O'Reilly, Jim O'Brien and Dennis O'Connor on a tweed and worsted
buying expedition to Donegal in the late 1950s.

workroom for 'Junior Miss' dresses (the teenage size) and later another workroom for 'Mademoiselle' dresses, the shorter, rather fuller, figure which seemed to be a French type.

Pauline Keller (Mrs Clotworthy) had called to see the managing director of Arnotts in 1938 after training in cutting and dressmaking in London. As there was no opening in Milne Models it was suggested that she open a school for dress design; this she did, the Grafton Academy, which has been ever since a strong influence in the development of dressmaking skill in the Republic. One of her teachers was Audrey Harrison (Mrs Howard) who in 1948 became assistant to Meta Soraghan (Mrs Dennehy) in Arnotts' Mademoiselle workroom, working for Miss Lee, buyer of dresses.

In 1950, Arnotts' maintenance manager, Cecil Clark, who had been given supervision of all workrooms, sent for Audrey Harrison. In her words:

> After a barrage of questions he appointed me to the Junior Miss workroom which was in Abbey Street. When Kitty Cassidy in 1951 took over this trade in a new Junior Miss department we formed an excellent working relationship. I used to design junior dresses specially for [fashion] parades and we would then make up a limited number of each which she sold exclusively in her department.
>
> In 1953 I moved to Milne Models combining my staff with theirs to produce all the brand names mentioned together with a Milne Model major range of larger sizes which were very successful up to the time I left to be married in 1958.

As taste is expressed in painting or music, so it is seen in the way clothes are worn. In Western civilisation, the best clothes show a basic simplicity related to the figure of the wearer, however elaborate the ornamentation may be, and very often the feeling of the moment is expressed in some detail such as scarf or bag. It is summed up in the word 'fashion' and an amount of nonsense is written about it. In setting up workrooms about the year 1950 Arnotts was working from the premise that its business was making and marketing clothing that fitted comfortably, looked good and lasted well. That is the basis of fashion.

In 1948, the designer, Dior, hit the market with an explosion of rich materials and lavish styles. After the squared shoulders and shorter 'pencil slim' skirts of the war period his 'new look' came as a tonic to the clothing trade – a brilliant anticipation of the feeling of the moment.

In that year, too, an exhibition of French post-Impressionist paintings was mounted in Dublin and Harry Dillon dressed ten windows in Arnotts, naming one for each of the post-Impressionist painters, with a large pastiche of his style as a backing to the clothes.[2] Cezanne's, for example, was a grouping of strong colour round a white tablecloth, which was as rigid as a misshapen bath, and the sales message, 'Put on colour with Cezanne'. At the time the tablecloth seemed wrong, but on a later trip to Paris one saw the picture which had inspired the pastiche – just like the corner of a bath!

So colour and excitement was coming back into the clothing trade as Europe struggled to its feet again, and Arnotts' total retail sales rose from £1.058 million in 1948 to £1.840 million in 1960, exceeding wholesale sales for the first time.

Con O'Shea, who came to Arnotts from Cork in 1957, had doubled the furniture trade by the year 1960. Only twenty-six years of age, he quickly realised the limitations of the local industry. The first post-war Earls Court Furniture Exhibition in London was a revelation. Instead of mahogany and walnut, new use was being made of teak, light oak, natural ash, yew, cherrywood; in upholstery, brighter colours had replaced conservative browns and greys. Despite import duty and levy, he found it necessary to import furniture. The new displays of G Plan and Ercol caused great excitement and interested Irish

---

[2]In 1948, Arnotts' electrical engineer recommended a new engine for the store's 70 volt system. With display in mind management rejected this idea and instead changed over to the ESB to make sure of adequate lighting.

manufacturers. Con O'Shea then set himself not only to foster the development of design in Ireland, but also to recruit and train a very good sales staff. For years, its leading member was Andrew Murray who was first salesman in Arnotts to achieve sales of over £100,000 in the year. He was later the first to achieve £500,000. Murray never seemed to be absent from his most prominent sales position on the furniture floor.

Con O'Shea has done more than anyone to complete the image Arnotts sought to present to Irish shoppers. He also married 'from stock', running the gauntlet of our sales-women to find his beautiful redhead wife, Kay Reale, in our suit department at the very back of the ground floor.

By 1960 too, John Golden, also from Cork, who started in 1956, had more than doubled our sale of shoes by opening a separate department for men's shoes. The number of retail departments had grown from 27 in 1948 to 35. Two other newcomers to buying were Tom Murray, who had returned to Arnotts from Todd Burns to buy carpets, and George Misstear who came from McBirneys to buy furnishing materials – these two replaced George Crampton who resigned from these two departments in 1952 to open his own successful business. Murray, in particular, had greatly increased sales of carpets by a policy of matching voluntarily the lower margins imposed on the clothing departments during the Emergency, but these two buyers complemented O'Shea's furniture to produce a strong 'house furnishing' division.

Winifred Gorry, when asked if there was anyone else like herself working in Dublin, without hesitation introduced Majella Gleeson who had been a supplier of goods made of Winifred Gorry's original felt material. In 1951 Majella Gleeson was invited to open a homecraft department based partly on the old 'Berlin' trade and partly on new do-it-yourself crafts; she was, of course, eminently fitted by experience and ability for the pioneering work this entailed.

Refugees from Europe added their skills to the existing pool of Irish knowledge. Arnotts' buyer, William Cummins, remembered in particular those who came from Hungary

The O'Dearest cartoon advertisements by Alan Warner featured city celebrities throughout the 1950s. William Nesbitt was a well-known chrysanthemum grower

after the invasion of 1956. They offered handcrafted lamps, candlesticks and other ornaments of which Arnotts bought quantities. Some of these refugees were able to move on to America with the money they made by selling these goods.

John Doody, who had his initial training in Lee and Co., joined Arnotts in 1948 in the man's shop. A year later he was appointed ADM in one of the successor departments to the old retail hosiery department of Paddy O'Flaherty – men's knitwear. By 1952 he was appointed buyer of this department and also of the neighbouring men's outfitting department and only a year later he was promoted to retail sales manager. Doody had very rapidly proved that his energy and personality fitted him for a wide-ranging role in the rapid development of Arnotts' retail trade. He adopted with alacrity the policy of increasing the number of retail departments – his own men's knitwear went to his ADM, Michael O'Dwyer, his outfitting to a newcomer, Derek Walshe (after a six months' hitch over union membership). Magda Payne and Eileen O'Driscoll took over newly created departments for handbags and gloves.

John Doody's appointment followed also from change at board level. Monsell had retired as company secretary in 1947 to be succeeded by Joseph Trevor, a very alert and conscientious retail office manager, who held the position for only two years before his early death in 1949. Leslie Montgomery, until then wholesale office manager, succeeded him.

Leslie Montgomery had started in Arnotts at the end of the First World War and was about as old as the century. With his hard wholesale office training in Arnotts, and his natural modesty, Montgomery made an excellent and loyal company secretary. He was no accountant and relied on the generous help given by Michael Manley of Craig Gardner, something beyond the call of duty considering that in 1951 it was agreed to raise the audit fee for the following year to a modest £200. That might be considered to amount to £4,000 in 1993's value. It is just one of those costs which does not compare with today's because of the requirements of successive Company Acts and the increasing and probably fruitless clamour for ultimate security.

In 1951 the board appointed the author joint managing director with his father, William, to take special interest in the developing retail side of the business. William Nesbitt never seemed to flag in his energy and enthusiasms but at sixty-seven age imperceptibly takes its toll. In fact, every other director, except Patrick O'Connor, had passed the age of sixty. The admirable retired secretary, Monsell, resigned as director in 1955 and died five years later at the age of ninety.

In 1957, with profits steady for some years at over £50,000 and dividend up to 20 per cent on the £4 ordinary shares, these ordinary shares were converted into four £1 shares to which a bonus issue of 2 for 1 was added. Thus the ordinary issued capital became £300,000. Preference shareholders were compensated for loss of priority in any liquidation by being issued with one bonus share for each two £1 preference shares held after the conversion into £1 denomination of the old £4; thus the preference capital became £90,000.

With so much at stake in Henry Street it became imperative to preserve industrial peace. When wartime restrictions on wage rises were removed, trade unions became more active again. Claims for increased rates of pay were presented by the Distributive Workers' Union and the No. 15 branch of the ITGWU to the drapery branch of the Federated Union of Employers. This was the largest of the FUE branches at the time. At the outset of a claim a general meeting of representatives of the employers was crowded into a first floor room in Fitzwilliam Street.

The main threat to peace in the drapery trade in Dublin in the 1950s arose from the fact that many shops and small stores employed few men, and resented claims which originated mostly among the men employed in the larger stores with which their staff, they said, were not so much concerned. Their representatives therefore started by talking strongly against any concessions, using time-worn phrases such as 'The Thin Edge of the Wedge' and 'Leave No Stone Unturned' in resisting the claim.

Unfortunately, there were some prominent men on the larger employers' side who were also hot enough under the collar to talk rather strongly and give encouragement to the right wing element of small employers. It was not unusual for a 'big' man like Denis Guiney to indulge himself in such talk, although one was fairly sure he had no wish to see the staff of Clery & Co. out on the street. There were, however, two very level heads who attended regularly: Laurence Cassidy (senior) and Patrick Bolger. The author, for Arnotts, always made the mistake of showing his hand too early in the meeting and would then have to sit willing Cassidy or Bolger to pour oil on the troubled waters as the time for lunch approached. This almost invariably happened, and the negotiating committee was authorised to negotiate.

From the names mentioned it will be seen that a number of new men had emerged in the drapery trade between the two world wars who had not been members of the old Merchant Drapers' Association. The McGuires, who had revived Clerys in the 1920s, were of the older order. Edward McGuire, senator and very reasonable gentleman, had been immediately elevated to the presidency of the FUE and in that position was no longer able to influence in any open way proceedings in the drapery branch.

Martin Winston of South Great Georges Street was one of these new men, and his son Martin accepted for a while the rather thankless task of chairman of the drapery branch.

Others like Tom Slowey and later Ben Dunne (Senior), after he had come from Cork to Henry Street, did not join, but took a keen interest in the branch's proceedings, criticising irritably at a distance as if they enjoyed some sort of associate membership.

In the early days of the FUE, before it grew larger, the drapery branch meetings were attended by one of its top officials, often by the director-general himself. The staff of the FUE were soon seen to be adopting a professional approach which had been lacking in the part-time secretaries of the older 'associations' of employers; it was reassuring to feel that they, like the secretaries of the employees' unions, wanted settlements, not strikes.

If, then, no one really wanted trouble the most obvious danger in the drapery trade came from the branches of the

Irish Transport and General Workers' Union, in particular the No. 15 branch which was strongly organised in the larger retail and wholesale firms. The members of the Transport Union watched jealously any advantage gained by the Distributive Workers and were, of course, determined to achieve the same. Stores such as Arnotts, with a large number of porters, packers and drivers were very sensitive to their feelings; smaller stores, such as Kellett's, had only a few transport workers, with whom they probably had a satisfactory long-term relationship. Their lack of concern with the demands of the Transport Union was always a cause of worry.

At this period, demands for more money came at intervals of years and were not a constant pre-occupation of management. It was also easy to assess, after a couple of meetings, and with another ear to the ground, what settlement could be reached. After the strike of 1939 Arnotts management had decided it did not wish to have another. Was it possible then in building a business to be a pacifist in industrial relations?

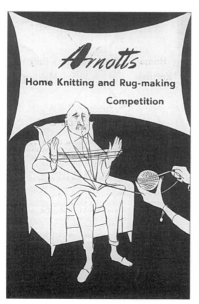

Arnotts' knitting competition in 1955 was a great success. Male entrants could also compete to win £15 for a sleeveless garment.

11 THE BALLET STORY

by Joan Lawler

IN AUGUST 1944 supplies of all kinds of goods had become increasingly difficult to obtain. Doris Cooney, buyer of Arnotts' retail corset department, discovered that her regular supplier of bras had run into financial and other difficulties. She brought her problem to the Manager. He had a name, of course, – William Nesbitt, Chairman and Managing Director of Arnotts but everyone called him 'The Manager'. His solution to the problem was typical: 'We'll make them ourselves.'

The supplier, Mrs Buchalter, had no licence to manufacture, or for that purpose to buy cloth. She existed by buying linen retail in Arnotts by the piece or even in the form of napkins and tablecloths. Arnotts employed her to design the bras, paid her £20 for her stock and two treadle machines, and undertook to sell to her husband at cost for re-sale 50 per cent of the production of what now became Arnotts' No. 3 Workroom.[1] We had the designer and two machinists and managed to meet the demands of the retail corset department. After the war the Buchalters re-started their own factory and ran it successfully for years.

One of the two original machinists, Mrs Elizabeth (Lil) Murphy, proved invaluable. She helped us to cut and grade patterns and recruited, trained and disciplined new staff. Established manufacturers were on suppliers' books and were offered a percentage of their pre-war purchases. We were unknown and had to scavenge for materials. We used anything we could find – cotton sheets, parachute

---

[1]*RN notes:* We had foolishly given numbers to our six workroom-factories. Initials are not much better. Names are always more memorable.

silk, any fabric we could buy retail. Hacksaw blades filed down were used as corset steels.

We approached Elliotts, a firm of poplin weavers in the Liberties. Their fabric was hand-woven and used for men's neckties and scarves. The width of the fabric was about 18–21 inches. We asked them if they could supply us with the cloth and dye it 'Tearose', which at the time was the only acceptable colour for corsets and bras. Elliotts were delighted and we could not believe our luck in having regular suppliers. Eventually, of course, the whole world was open to us. Sadly, Elliotts' weavers were older men and no young people appeared anxious to learn this old craft. The firm closed, but we remember them as our first regular suppliers.

Production expanded and exceeded Doris Cooney's needs. We asked Arnotts' wholesale if they were interested. They were indeed. Production increased again and by 1948 we were making more than demanded by Arnotts' retail and wholesale divisions. Arnotts' travellers carried samples from every department ranging from blankets and men's suits to needles and thread. Their customer in each town was the largest general draper; not necessarily the best outlet for bras. There was little incentive for the traveller to push the sales of bras, when he could sell higher-priced items like linens or outerwear.

Obviously, No. 3 Workroom had to do some market research. A car was provided for us to travel the country and confirm that alternative outlets for bras existed. The response was overwhelming. Every shop visited placed an order. We could not supply these accounts as 'Arnotts' because they were not all Arnotts' customers. The Manager produced an off the shelf company and No. 3 Workroom became Walter Edwards Ltd. in August 1948, a wholly owned subsidiary of Arnotts. We recruited a second commercial traveller and registered the brand name 'Ballet'.

We were still working in Henry Street, but by the early 1950s no more space was available. Before the Second World War Arnotts had bought two Georgian houses in Upper Dominick Street and built a warehouse, two storeys over basement, to carry any stocks they could obtain before the wartime shortages bit. This warehouse was now empty except for the basement, which housed Arnotts' fleet of delivery vans. In 1953 Walter Edwards Ltd. moved about a quarter of a mile up the road into this building.

We were making blouses, children's dresses and sun-bonnets. We had long abandoned our treadle machines and embarked on a programme of buying the best machinery available. On the only occasion we consulted the Manager about a new and rather expensive machine his typical reply was: 'Are you sure you don't need two of them? Buy whatever you want. Run the place as if it were your own.' What a far seeing, open minded and encouraging man he was, and what loyalty, commitment and affection he commanded. Within twelve months another storey had been added to the Dominick Street building and we asked Arnotts for the use of the basement.

Ireland in 1957 was in deep recession. Duty on imported garments, hitherto 60 per cent, was increased by a levy. Few foreign companies could compete with this. An English manufacturer of foundation garments – Gossard Ltd., whose single largest Irish outlet was Arnotts' retail corset department – asked Arnotts to recommend an Irish manufacturer to produce their brand for the Irish market. Walter Edwards could and would.

One-third of the equity of Walter Edwards was sold to Gossard who agreed to give Walter Edwards sole right to manufacture and distribute Gossard for the Irish market. To meet the demands of both Ballet and Gossard, we ceased production of blouses and bonnets and became 100 per cent manufacturers of foundation garments.[2]

Unhappily, around 1961, ill-health forced Mrs Murphy to resign. This led us to make two appointments. Miss Betty Fallon was promoted to replace Lil Murphy and we employed an industrial engineer, Jim Power, as production manager. These two people, then in their twenties, formed

---

[2] *RN notes:* The decision to abandon the successful manufacture of blouses under the name 'Vanity Fair' was surprisingly courageous, showing a clear-cut appreciation of where the factory's future lay.

Inside the factory: (standing from right) B. Hatfield, designer, Joan Lawler (managing director), Betty Fallon (factory manager)

the nucleus of the management team which transformed Walter Edwards into an internationally competitive company. Without the commitment, hard work, and energy of Jim Power and Betty Fallon, Ballet might well have ceased growing.[3]

We grew in strength and changed the company name to 'Ballet International'. In the 1960s the buzz word was export; we did, until 60 per cent of our production was going out of the country. With growth like this we needed more space. First Arnotts bought three adjoining Georgian houses and on their site extended our existing building to 30,000 square feet. We then rented a further 10,000 square feet nearby to accommodate our warehouse and dispatch. In 1972 we made the decision to move our operation into a custom built factory of 62,400 square feet in the Finglas Industrial Estate. The move into our new single storey premises was completed in August 1976.

With the gradual dismantling of duties within the EEC we suggested to Courtaulds, who had taken over a year after our association with Gossard, that they resume exporting to Ireland. They were delighted but agreed with great reluctance to our demand for a royalty of 7.5 per cent on all their Irish sales.

This gave us freedom to develop our own Ballet range which now needed the space and skills we had been giving to Gossard. Towards the end of the 1970s we bought back Courtaulds' share of the company and we were once again a wholly owned subsidiary of Arnotts.

Ballet International never stopped growing and never showed a loss in its forty-three year history. Over the years it contributed appreciably to the profits of the Arnotts group. Sadly, however, in 1987 Arnotts decided to sell Ballet. In that year its sales exceeded £5 million. It

---

[3]In April 1988 Jim Power, director of Ballet International, and Peter Lynott, sales manager, decided to start production on their own account and have been trading since as Sapphire Lingerie Ltd. They were joined in June 1988 by Betty Fallon.

continues to this day as the Irish part of a Swedish inter-national group.[4]

The cover of a 1957 Ballet sales brochure

---

[4]Muiris Heron, financial manager, returned to Henry Street in September 1988. He had started in Arnotts in 1967 and was seconded to Ballet in 1978 as accountant. There had been setbacks in establishing satisfactory accounting, owing to rapid development and very frequent changes of accounting staff. Heron found the going difficult at first, but despite the additional growing pains of computerisation left behind him sound controls, satisfactory budgeting, and reliable reporting. He is now chief accountant in the Arnotts group.

Arnotts' staff pension fund continues to hold preserved pensions for four executive staff of Ballet because no satisfactory alternative fund was available.

12 *ANDANTE CON BRIO* 1960–1970

THE CHAIRMAN TOLD the annual general meeting of March 1961 that the rebuilding of numbers 7–10 Henry Street was 'fairly complete'. In 1957 he had declared that he saw no prospect of population growth 'in the fore-seeable future' (sic), and in 1958 with conscious humour said: 'Shareholders who scrutinise our annual accounts, and I hope many do, will as a rule find little variation in our figures; not surprising perhaps in an economy such as we enjoy where the tempo may be scored *andante.*' No wonder he was loath to spend more than £100,000 on 7–10 Henry Street.

In the next ten years *andante* became at least *con brio*, and if the population of the state showed little increase, it became more concentrated in Dublin and in Henry Street. In 1961, profit after tax exceeded £100,000 for the first time and three years later was over £200,000.

The dividend rate had reached 20 per cent in 1955 and in 1962 had again, after the 1958 splitting of shares into £1 denomination and the 2 for 1 bonus issue, reached 20 per cent on the increased capital of £300,000. That left enough taxed profit to reserve to replace the £250,000 spent on building in less than five years. Between 1960 and 1970 retail sales increased at a steady rate from £1.8 million to £5.2 million showing net profits of over 10 per cent almost every year. The enlarged Henry Street building, most of the basement having been cleared of wholesale depart-ments and café to make a retail 'lower ground floor', was filled by expanding previously cramped departments. The number of retail departments increased from thirty-five to forty. The length of window display in Henry Street had grown by half. The whole ground floor back to the Prince's Street/Proby Lane axis, apart from a corner taken by a new high-pressure steam boiler, was devoted to retail trade. Most of the balcony level, carried through to the party wall of 7 Henry Street, was filled by the new larger café with its elaborate preparation areas and kitchen.

This rebuilding of the entire sites of 7–8 Henry Street cleared all the rambling, rat-infested building behind the old Georgian frontage. It had been necessary in the fur workrooms to clad the walls of the cold store with metal up to a height of 15 inches to keep out these vermin. The rat-catchers, as the men were more simply named in those days, proved less than fully effective, to judge by a story told by Ella Nesbitt. She was sitting in her car in Prince's Street one evening when Tommy Murphy, assistant to Paddy Murphy in the transport department, came trotting down the street, the words tumbling over one another from his mouth: 'Mrs Ranny, Mrs Ranny, roll up your windows, the rats is coming!' Next moment rats came running out of the door from the basement, pursued by the rat-catcher along the street until they peeled off into Woolworth's basement. Well, you cannot really expect a man to put himself out of a job; Arnotts did it by rebuilding.

The purchase of Naylors' old furniture store, which had blocked Arnotts' outlet to Liffey Street, provided another goods entrance which was devoted to the growing furniture trade and to supplies for the café and work-rooms.

The original 1937 café, under its manageress, Miss O'Brien, had made considerable sales: £39,000 in its last complete year, 1958. It had to be closed because its whole kitchen area was in the basements of 7–10 Henry Street, which were also to be rebuilt. Miss O'Brien left before the rebuilding and the staff accepted due notice with the undertaking that they would have priority when the new café was opened.

The old kitchen was managed by male chefs whose regime was based on the cutting and preparing of meat. This led to the production of excellent roasts and steaks;

they obviously cared less for fish, which was not always unquestionably fresh.

Since it was hoped to make the new café less of a restaurant, and the kitchen staff more amenable to management by a woman, the choice of women cooks was obvious. Fortunately, Julia Kennedy, who had run the lunchroom at the Department of Lands, was available to undertake the task, and she brought with her in time for the opening her trusted head cook, May Daly. With steam available to the café from the boiler which had been installed in the new building primarily for the pressing work of the men's tailoring, shirt and dress factories on the upper floors, steam could be used for everything except the ovens and grills which used gas.

Self-service was the original plan, but in the end the L shape of the customer areas, which allowed exit from the kitchen on two sides, had waitress service along the Henry Street windows with self-service along the balcony overlooking the ground floor of the store. The balance in favour of providing waitress service at the opening of the new café had been tipped by a special worry: what would the nuns think? In the old café, a corner behind the stairs had been curtained off for them.

At the time, Arnotts was a little apologetic about self-service so the best silver-plated cutlery, teapots and jugs from Newbridge, and everything else to match, were used throughout. In the first full year of trading, sales in the new café were double those reached in the last year of the old; by 1973 sales were over £300,000; the café was then changed completely to self-service and five years later sales of £900,000 had been reached.

This abandonment of waitress service was forced by the difficulty of staffing, despite the efforts of excellent waitresses like May Rafferty and Rita Mitchell. The work in a busy service area, allowing no more than fourteen 'covers' for each waitress, became impossible when holidays and unexpected sickness reduced the number of waitresses from the full twelve to nine or even fewer; if customers shouting for service were to be avoided the surplus tables had to be stripped from the room until, with its green and white floor,

The front of the store in the 1960s

A busy scene in the interior of the store in the early 1960s – note the nuns in pre-Vatican II habits!

it looked like a deserted field. Fortunately, by now most nuns no longer wore long black habits and proved, if anything, more capable of managing trays than many lay customers. Even men proved able to carry trays, though some to this day are content to wait while their patient wives carry their food to their tables.

Julia Kennedy was a demanding manager, duly impatient and successful in running for over twenty-five years what was, in effect, a very busy food factory; she was absolutely loyal to her own staff, in particular to the kitchen staff who do not often enjoy the limelight. One of the most genuine tributes to her may not be the one she most desires to see in print. It came from Charlie Dunne, maintenance manager, who was as sardonically witty as any Dubliner can be! When asked what holidays he had, he said, 'Well, there are two weeks when I'm away, (pause) and there are two weeks when Miss Kennedy is away.'

Like any factory, the café had more need of maintenance than other trading departments. Dunne turned his remark into the greatest possible compliment from him by adding, 'I'll grant her this, she knows what she's there for.' Julia Kennedy, whose younger sister, Clair, became buyer of our jewellery department from 1975 onwards, until marriage proved more attractive, is proud of her family's record in Arnotts and her work as senior manager of our cafés – she acted as consultant to our cafés in Boyers and in Grafton Street. Her final service to Arnotts was to provide a very competent successor in Joyce Sheridan, another energetic and determined redhead.

The increase in the number of retail departments in the late 1950s brought more women fashion buyers. Mrs Josephine Carolan bought women's coats, Elizabeth Heffernan model gowns, Kathleen Byrne corsets, Mary Foran dresses and in 1960 Mary Foran's friend, Evelyn Buggy, from the dress shop, Sheila's, in O'Connell Street, came to buy women's suits, when Kitty Cassidy (Mrs Crossan) left Arnotts to become 'Madam Nora' of O'Connell Street. Kitty Cassidy's Junior Miss department had been closed 'for the present at any rate' because current thinking was opposed to any possible duplication of stocks; she had been a little too successful in attracting juniors of all ages. Today such internal competition in the store is considered healthy; it helps to avoid gaps in stock. With Maureen Lynch already buying separates, Winifred Gorry hats and jewellery and Nancy O'Grady the beauty shop, Arnotts had a strong fashion team.

Among the men in retail, Denis Hannigan was managing silks with his own brand of very neat competence and Jim O'Brien had introduced splendidly up-market ranges of French woollens.

Retirements also brought change; Hugh Neary, who had started in Arnotts in 1916, retired through ill-health in 1960 and Paddy Murphy of the transport department, who had joined in 1904, retired in 1961. Their pensions were among the first paid by the new pension fund for which the trustees were the author, Tennyson Lee and Jim Hughes chosen by the directors of Arnotts, and Patrick Walsh of the furnishing department and Larry O'Dwyer of the wages office nominated by the members. Hugh Neary's important retail and wholesale linen departments were taken over by John Tierney and Thomas Walsh respectively.

Captain Tennyson Lee of Edward Lee and Son had been co-opted to Arnotts' board in 1958 in the hope that a closer link with Lee's shops stretching across the population centres of South County Dublin might be developed. He was in any case a welcome addition since he shared completely Arnotts' outlook.

The original Sun Life of Canada pension scheme had been closed in 1958, when a sum of £80,000 was handed over to the new trustees of Arnotts' staff pension fund with a list of the amount standing to credit of each current member; those who had already started to draw pensions continued to be paid by Sun Life, and in all cases Arnotts supplemented, ex gratia, pensions considered inadequate because of the short twenty-year history of the fund to date.

Forty years ago, few sought retirement: it was considered a death sentence. Having worked a five and a half day week of 44 hours, before the Second World War, shortened officially by closing at 5.30 p.m. during the war, and unofficially by extending the lunch hour break, most became rooted in Henry Street. Except perhaps in summer, free time was a short weekend for housekeeping and church-going. If work justifies, this was their justification; they could ill afford, and had no wish, to leave their daily companions behind.

Eileen O'Callaghan, for example, was an energetic sales-woman, becoming dependent on the support of her fellow saleswomen in the dresses department. She said of retire-ment: 'What will I do? I'll miss the other girls so much.' Mary McCaffrey, on the other hand, leading sales in women's hats, retired at Christmas 1959 without plaint; she had started in Arnotts in 1908, was bright-eyed and bustling in manner and loved hats. She declared she could always sell a hat even when the customer brought a friend into the fitting room; but two friends made things impossible because the two always took opposite sides in any question of taste. We then designed fitting rooms to hold no more than one friend. In 1993 the space has been renamed 'changing room' and holds one only – no friends.

In the period 1960-70 wholesale sales increased from £1.8 million to over £3 million – not as strong a performance as Henry Street retail. Four of the seventeen departments had been abandoned or had been amalgamated with others – notably the wholesale boot trade, and rayon and woollen materials; the latter fell victim to the decline of piece goods in favour of ready-to-wear garments. A new department for babywear, under Campbell Heather, had emerged to keep the number at fourteen.

The buying team remained largely unchanged but Kevin Lawless, son of Martin Lawless, took over shirts and the shirt factory on Hanley's retirement in 1962 and developed it steadily until in 1968 he decided to change career to a branch of metal manufacturing; this move was possibly decided in part by the tragic death of his young wife, Eileen Wall. She was one of Arnotts' outstanding prizewinners in the School of Retail Distribution and (to quote Jim Hughes) had been so good a member of his wholesale team that she was poached by our retail, becoming assistant manager to Eileen O'Driscoll in the children's department.

French Festival 1969: (above) Ella and Ronald Nesbitt greet M. André de Viggiani (below) a window – note the prices in francs!

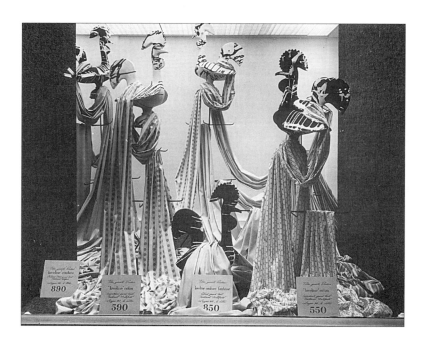

In 1965, Tom Tunney took over and greatly expanded the men's ready-to-wear department; sales increased to five times those of 1960 with much improved stock-turn and margins of profit. In the same year, Ross Dallas, who had taken over Heather's children's coat department in 1959, persuaded Arnotts to bring into the top floor along Henry Street the troubled manufacturing organisation of his main supplier. This trebled the children's coat trade in this period. Other very strong performances came in women's knitwear and skirts, bought by Eddie Keogh, and neckwear by Tommy Lonergan.

Between 1960 and 1970 the consumer price index rose by 60 per cent; the wholesale division achieved growth of 66 per cent, so just managed to increase its volume of business thanks to the more successful departments; on the other hand, Arnotts' retail clearly outstripped the index by rising 189 per cent.

In April 1962 John Doody was appointed retail manager in Henry Street. Jim Hughes had been appointed whole-sale manager in 1958. The two general managers now had constant contact with the buyers – the managers of the trading departments – which was an immense gain. Both Doody and Hughes set up procedures of regular reporting of purchases and ideas for promoting sales at the beginning of trading seasons, as well as careful scrutiny of stocks to be cleared by the wonderfully swift stream of Arnotts' Sales in July and January.

Customers have often asked how it is possible to sell goods at half price, 'You must have an enormous profit.' The answer is that sales at half price are certainly without profit, but that at the end of a season 'half a loaf is better than no bread', if by bread is meant cash to reinvest in trading in the next period. Another function of Sales is to clear by additional orders materials and stocks of goods left in suppliers' hands as the season is coming to a close. These will show a small profit in the retailer's hand because the supplier has been able to achieve little or none. Arnotts had long enough experience of the deadening effect of carrying stocks because they were 'good'.

The wide variety of relatively highly priced goods carried

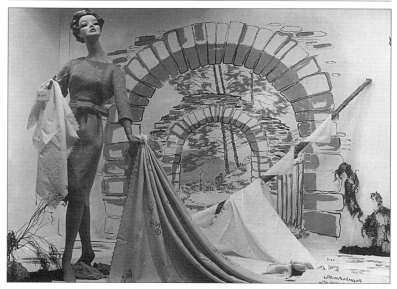

The decorated windows celebrating Irish Fortnight in October 1961

Chatting at a reception in Arnotts in 1961, (left to right) Ronald Nesbitt, H. Dillon (display manager) and John Doody (sales manager)

in a department store makes the rapid movement of stocks more difficult, and therefore all the more vital. It is sad to lose money, but tragic to lose your trade.

'French Festival at Arnotts' in October 1959, was Ireland's first presentation of a 'foreign fortnight'. On the other hand, in October 1961, 'Irish Fortnight at Arnotts' was so successful that the formula was used again in 1963 to promote one single commodity – Carberry Tweeds. 'Carberry Fortnight at Arnotts' was a great boost for the weaving industry in Clonakilty .

France was chosen for promotion again in 1964 but with a difference. The Pyrenean Region was a source of exclusive merchandise and the museum in Lourdes lent exhibits of interest to Irish people. The title of the event was 'French Fortnight and Pyrenean Exhibition at Arnotts'.

Ambassadors or government ministers opened the fort-nights. Other personalities appeared in the store during the run of the event. This suggested a new promotional activity of presenting celebrities.

Sir Matt Busby made a memorable visit, accompanied by Billy Behan, his Irish scout and esteemed friend. At a function in the store, guests included the British Ambassador, and members of the media. Sir Matt was due in the store at 2.30 p.m. to sign autographs. About half an hour before the time Henry Street was completely blocked by the crowds. In response to the clamour, 'We want Busby', he climbed on to the canopy overlooking Henry Street and there acknowledged the enthusiastic crowd. Soon he started signing autographs, personalising every one.

Alison Settle (woman's editor of the *Observer* news-paper), the footballer, Steve Heighway, and Christian Dior's beautiful Burmese model, Alla Illitchun, were other distinguished people who appeared in the store during the 1960s.

'American Fortnight at Arnotts' took place in October 1967. Five American Indians of the Shawnee tribe were a major attraction during this promotion. According to the Commerce Department in Washington, the event created a world record for publicity achieved during an American fortnight in any part of the world. The following October

William Nesbitt in 1966, after   Boyers in North Earl Street, which
his retirement   joined the Arnotts group in the
                                    1960s

Model Jean Shrimpton, one of the many celebrities who visited Arnotts,
being greeted at Dublin Airport in 1966 by John Doody (left) and
Vivian Dudgeon

'London Festival at Arnotts' was produced. According to the British Board of Trade, this too created a record for publicity relating to a British promotion .

In October 1968 events in Northern Ireland took a serious turn and an era of tragic and costly strife for the whole country was soon unleashed. Arnotts and other businesses were adversely affected. The company had to abandon promotional plans outlined in early 1968 for presentation in the following three or four years. Overseas personalities and business people were fearful of visiting Ireland. Consultants, advisors and product demonstrators cancelled visits. Happily, there were no outrages in Arnotts during the worst years and no one there suffered death or injury, but sadly the same could not be said of other parts of the city.

The situation improved in the mid-1970s but security had to remain a priority. Security in the department store is a costly business with its threefold responsibility for staff, shoppers and premises.

In mid-1960 William Nesbitt surprised his fellow directors with the information that he had been offered 83 per cent of the ordinary shares of Boyers Limited of North Earl Street. As usual, James Fagan (senior) and Major Alec Nesbitt, the conservative wing of the board, doubted the wisdom of moving across O'Connell Street. Patrick O'Connor, Tennyson Lee and the author were in favour. The author was able to convert his uncle with the very modest promise of profits of £5,000 a year from North Earl Street.

The managing director of Boyers, Ivan Hart, was strongly in favour of the change, since net profits in Boyers had virtually disappeared. Boyers' staff in meeting is said to have cheered the news.

It took a year to complete the change of ownership so the first half-year's figures are for autumn 1961 showing total sales of £72,000 with direct selling expenses of 13.7 per cent and little hope of meeting overhead costs. There were eleven departments and buyers, a number of whom proved to be winners. There was no shoe department so John Golden from Henry Street was asked to open one, thus becoming Arnotts' first retail group buyer. In the autumn of 1962 sales had risen in all departments to a total of £133,000 with direct expenses of 9 per cent and a net profit of 8.2 per cent. The corresponding figures for Henry Street were sales of nearly £1.4 million with direct expenses of 6.8 per cent and net profit of 12 per cent. Boyers was simply a business starved of capital – the management and team spirit were good.

By 1970, Boyers' sales had passed £1 million with direct expenses held steady at 8.9 per cent and a net profit of 6.7 per cent. There were twenty-one departments including a café. Twelve of the buyers from Henry Street were also buying for Boyers, mostly with new departments but a couple replacing buyers who had retired. Two of the splendid traders we found in Boyers, Mary Gaffney, buyer of coats, suits and dresses and Mrs Dorothy Hayes, buyer of hats, had retired because of age. Miss Gaffney distinguished herself by holding prayers in her department every Monday morning; to judge by her success alone it was a good idea.

To find room in Boyers for these added departments, in 1965 Arnotts bought 17 North Earl Street for £50,000 which also extended the frontage on the street and incorporated the open yard and neighbouring buildings on Cathedral Street to achieve a rectangular ground floor and a customer flow from street to street.

In 1964 Patrick O'Connor suggested buying the building of the jewellers, West's, in Grafton Street. William Nesbitt, who had retired as joint managing director in 1961 but remained as director and chairman until 1966, immediately opposed the idea, but said the following day that he would like the board to consider the suggestion. In June 1966 the building was bought at auction for £120,000 plus fees.

The conversion of the building cost as much again because of the immense job of digging the jeweller's massive strong room out of the basement, which had in addition to be 'tanked' to cope with the stream which surprisingly runs under Grafton Street. Conversion costs included extending the first floor from front to back of the building and resiting the front stairs with a new lift to all floors, before dismantling the old, for the convenience of the tenants on the top three floors.

Arnotts believed that it had goods and a service which would appeal to southside shoppers who did not cross the Liffey. This idea was supported by the weight of deliveries from Henry Street to the south of Dublin.[1]

The Grafton Street branch was opened in May 1966 with a near-riot caused by the presence of the English model, Jean Shrimpton. She had shot to fame in 1965 wearing the first mini-skirt at the races in Australia. She was sensational. At the opening in Grafton Street the crowds were swollen by the arrival of hundreds of students. There was an air of excitement, and male pressure to get closer to the celebrity became menacing.

The young men, in black leather breeches and jackets, were shouting 'Up, up!' and the Shrimp was hoisted on to one of the glass counters, so that her legs could be viewed to advantage. She was wearing a white tweed suit with a skirt about two inches above the knee – by no means today's mini-skirt. By that time a glass counter had been cracked by the pressure of the crowd; the staff pushed other counters back to clear some space and the Shrimp was led rapidly upstairs to the clearer space of the coats, suits and dresses area. The crowd downstairs waited for her to re-appear.

A council of war decided that Ella Nesbitt, who was wearing a coat of bawneen tweed looking vaguely like the suit worn by Jean Shrimpton, should ostentatiously exit by the back door into Wicklow Street while it was announced to the main crowd that the model had left by that way. Believing this, many ran round into Wicklow Street; in their disappointment came shouts of 'It's only the ould

---

[1]This may have been due to South Dubliners being more exacting about the free delivery service. When it was later discovered that a relative of one of Arnotts' directors had asked for a pair of gloves to be delivered home a charge of 10s was imposed. A minor charge is a wonderful test of real need. It is no harm to make virtue pay; this charge was 'given' to the sales of each department to make sure the staff imposed it. A very noticeable reduction in small parcels for delivery followed.

wan!' Jean Shrimpton escaped to safety, through the front door, and the new store turned to business.

The first complete half-year's trading in Grafton Street was that of autumn 1966, in which the twelve women's departments sold £182,000 with a direct expense averaging 11 per cent and a net profit of 5 per cent. The final stock at cost had risen by only £4,000 which made that result reasonably secure. The strongest departments were women's outerwear, separates and shoes; the first of these was bought by Joan McCrone, recruited as a young fashion buyer to placate William Nesbitt, who believed Grafton Street was a different area and needed a different team.

The other eleven were the tried team of group buyers from Henry Street to whom, except for Kate Murphy (lingerie) and Cyril Claffey (stockings), you have already been introduced. In 1970, Joan McCrone was still the only buyer based in Grafton Street, and Kevin Groarke had taken over stockings, Marie O'Rorke was in charge of gloves, Mary Tallon of novelties, Mary Brophy of jewellery and Majella Gleeson of lingerie.

By 1970, sales in Grafton Street were just short of £5 million with a direct staff cost of 9.8 per cent, a net profit of 6.1 per cent and a money turn of stock 7.5 times.

The general manager in this first period in Grafton Street was Vivian Dudgeon, who had come to Boyers from Ferrier Pollock in December 1959 as assistant manager. Though he had a carefully picked sales team, with particular importance given to the assistant manager in each department, who was to have near buyer status, Dudgeon deserves great credit for his achievement in launching this store.

The company secretary, Leslie Montgomery, surprised the board of Arnotts by insisting on retirement in early 1962 at the age of sixty-five. He explained that he had too much to do and was probably relieved to be rid of the position's very wide responsibility.[2] He had joined Arnotts

---

[2]The corners of his mouth were often white from chewing antacid tablets. But some things did not worry him. He enjoyed walking in Scotland and apparently nursed a secret desire to possess a Golden Eagle's egg. He was later fined in Scotland for achieving this hazardous ambition.

in 1914, served in the Royal Navy during the First World War, returning to Arnotts after the war. He was co-opted a director and retired in 1973 with the deliberate intention of creating a vacant place for Michael Nesbitt, great-grandson of Alexander.

Monty was replaced by John C. O'Sullivan, a university graduate and accountant, who not only had some experience in cloth manufacturing but also a background in the drapery trade; his grandfather had been chairman of Todd Burns & Co. of Mary Street.

James Fagan (Senior) died in 1964. He was every inch a cheerful rubicund Dubliner, a solicitor who never really came to terms with the sang-froid of business men in their dealings with one another. If asked to draw up a code of conduct he would almost certainly have suggested more resort to properly drawn legal agreements. Of course, a correctly executed and acknowledged order is a legal agreement, if the two parties to it are *ad idem*. James Fagan acted once for Arnotts in a case where this was not so. The ADM of Eddie McCourt's wholesale children's department placed, in McCourt's absence, an order for so many dozen dresses at 48s thinking they were splendid value for the dozen, which was the normal way for a manufacturer to quote a wholesale price. There was consternation when the invoices started to arrive priced at 48s each. Arnotts returned the consignments to the English manufacturer who sued in the Irish court and failed, because the parties were not of like mind. It was entirely possible to buy children's dresses at 48s a dozen at that date just after the Second World War.

James C. Fagan, nephew of the deceased, also a solicitor in the same practice, was co-opted in his uncle's place.

Tennyson Lee resigned as director in June 1964, pleading age. It is likely, however, that Edward Lee & Co. was now managed by younger members of the Lee family who had little inclination for a merger with Arnotts. The author, who had enjoyed a time as a director of Lee's, also resigned from Lee's board. The remorseless rise of costs was beginning to snap at the heels of the older and smaller department stores, despite their devotion to their family business. A business consultant addressing a meeting in the city of

Chief Wolf Robe and other Shawnees performing a Plains' Indian
ceremonial dance

Patrick O'Connor, Ronald Nesbitt and James Fagan (Junior) conferring
in 1967

Galway, criticised at length the dead hand of families in business. In Galway of all places! The chairman in 'thanking' him asked if one had to be a bit of a bastard to succeed in business. Business is a constant grind, one stands it better for being brought up to it.

In 1966 William Nesbitt resigned as a director and on his suggestion Jim Hughes was co-opted in his place. The author was elected chairman for the remainder of the business year.

At the end of 1967 Major Alec Nesbitt retired and Patrick J. O'Connor followed him at the end of the following year. Patrick O'Connor freely gave regular advice on building, shopfitting and all the physical aspects of Arnotts' business, including ready valuations of property. He formed the face of Arnotts presented to Dublin at that time – it was true to say of him, *Si monumentum requeris circumspice*. He was replaced on the board by his son, Michael, architect and barrister, who, knowing in detail the history of our buildings was well fitted to take up the task laid down by his father.

In 1966 the question of industrial relations again had to be faced. A very long spell of negotiations with the Distributive Workers' Union, which involved recasting the office scale completely, did not produce an offer of increased money. Staff in Arnotts and Switzers lost patience and voted in each case to make a demand on management for an extra £2 a week. Switzers asked the drapery branch of the FUE to support them in resisting this claim. The danger was a return to an old two tier scale.

Arnotts thought the trade might laugh at this demand and did not ask for support. The chairman of Arnotts' house committee at the time was a personable young man who was employed as a porter but had, most unusually, been admitted to the Distributive Workers' Union; with a couple of friends he persuaded a rather inexperienced house committee to promote this demand and stimulated a meeting of the staff to vote in favour of it. No separate wage claims had been made by the Distributive Workers' Union on an individual store since the establishment of the FUE.

Arnotts wrote an incautiously irate letter to Michael Fitzpatrick, secretary of the Distributive Union, who had been a salesman in Arnotts' carpet department and was highly regarded by Arnotts. Fitzpatrick asked us to confirm if he should put the letter before the union executive. Having cooled a bit, Arnotts thanked him and withdrew the letter.

As tactfully as possible, Arnotts refused the claim and another meeting of the staff voted to press it. Why not, if there was nothing to lose? So the question had been put. Must one give way for the sake of peace? Could peace be bought? The directors were kept fully informed and sympathised with the dilemma facing the executives: to refuse the claim and risk a strike or to make some settlement and buy another period of peace, thereby risking what has since become known as its 'credibility'. A strike would destroy, for a period at least, the goodwill that had been built over years; this would then have to be rebuilt.

The decision was to stand firm against the demand, offering instead to put into immediate effect the new office scale and other items that had been agreed by the FUE drapery branch. The managing director, with Jim Hughes and John Doody, put this before a specially convened meeting of Arnotts' house committee; from memory about eighteen staff attended and made little comment. At the crucial meeting of the staff some of Arnotts' managers made a strong stand against the proposed strike and it was decisively rejected. When the officers of the house committee came, rather downcast, to report this decision, they were amazed to realise that management intended in any event to honour its promise to put the new office scale and other items into immediate effect. The bond between management and staff had not been broken.

13 BEHIND THE SCENES AT
   ARNOTTS 1940–1970

IN 1962, WITH THE appointment of John O'Sullivan as new-style company secretary, the group's accounting became professional rather than devotedly amateur. William Nesbitt's eve of retirement 'bequest' of an IBM computer model 360/20 was an agent of that change from 1966.

Until then, there had always been a tendency for shop and office to blame one another for unpleasant surprises in financial results. Even after the introduction of the stock control system in 1939, and the early refinement of departmental accounting in 1945 by the complete separation of wholesale from retail, sales staff were all too ready to blame stock shortages on mistakes in the office. In fact, the office was more often right.

Recurring shortages reported by stock control over ten years, increasing in size at the end of that period, was one of the causes of the resignation of the furniture buyer in 1957. After his departure it was discovered that one of his trusted staff had been regularly helping himself to the department's cash. It is much easier for a bad penny on the staff to make away with the money than it is for the shoplifter to 'lift' the goods. But, since we hate to think badly of our friends, we ignore what the shortages are suggesting. It is too easy to blame shoplifters for disappointing figures, as happened at one period in our handbag department. Handbags, it was thought, were asking to be slipped on the shoulder on the way out of the store. A count of the stock, morning and evening for a whole twelve months, produced a total of only fourteen missing bags.

Rita Canning of accounts demonstrating the NCR ledger posting machinery

Tommy Murphy, assistant manager of the transport department, who 'saved' Ella Nesbitt from the rats

Joe Clery (left) and members of the accounts department (including Rita Canning). Note the old high desk.

Until the 1960s most records were kept in solidly bound books, hand written, though no longer by clerks standing, sometimes on duckboard, at long sloping counters. Reporting by trading departments was still on large ruled sheets. The retail sheet measured 21 x 19 inches with 31 columns; the wholesale sheet of the same width was only 12 inches long with 29 columns. Written up painstakingly and beautifully by John Young, with the figures of the year before in red ink above the black figures of the half year just passed, and a black line under each batch of three departments to guide the eye of the reader, they were, in their way, works of art.

The number of columns was largely dictated by the stock control at selling price and the figures it generated, such as estimated gross profit. After computerisation of the stock control these figures became available to the buyers for the first time on a continuous basis so that the stock control clerk became their confidant and guide. This was the point at which general management, through the monthly sheet which was on the same lines as the half-yearly, came into closer financial contact with the trading. Not only the competence but also the personality of the control clerk was of unusual importance.

John Byrne carried this responsibility until 1967 when he became an assistant to the company secretary in general office management. Jack Moore then took over the work and, after years of adjustment and refinement due to computerisation, is still master of the system in 1993. The computer's output is now presented monthly in book form, and each buyer gets a copy of the page of figures for his or her own department.

The additional space provided by the new 7–10 Henry Street building in 1961 allowed the high tide of selling departments to recede leaving space free on the first floor of Henry Street old front for offices. The general counting house continued to separate into its component parts and spread into the rooms available.

The purchasing office, under Joe O'Reilly, assumed a distinct identity, which was good for morale. Aidan Kelly, who took over on O'Reilly's retirement, is still in charge today and Pauline Murray is still a member of his band.[1]

Until 1964, in striking contrast with the divisional and departmental accounting, the directors' annual report and statement of accounts was still on the 16 x 10¼ inches sheet of white paper folded over to make four pages of which the 'cover' page was the notice of the annual general meeting, page two the directors' report and page three the profit and loss account and the balance sheet. At the bottom of page three, Craig Gardner's report was of four lines. The back page had nothing but the rather beautiful seal of the company. Of course, this neat format omitted a great deal of detail which is elaborated in the colourful reports of today, in eight times as many pages, not counting the cover.[2]

The six-monthly wholesale and retail sheets contained an abundance of detail, but general managers had to wait patiently for other information. Andrew McGorlick, of the wages' office, was unable to produce reports of six-monthly sales by assistants and of days lost through sickness without considerable delay, which was not surprising since he had only a clumsy mechanical totting machine to assist him.[3] He was a cheerful, immensely hardworking man, with an encyclopedic knowledge of the staff, most of whom were still paid weekly in cash. He enjoyed life, featuring in many photographs of outings of Arnotts' Golfing Society.

Laurence (Larry) O'Dwyer, who joined Arnotts in 1937, was McGorlick's successor. He continued the tradition of close detailed interest in all the activities of staff, acting as their recorder and photographer as well as their counsellor. He was naturally proposed by the members of the staff

---

[1] Those who know Pauline will understand the use of the word 'band'; she is a very pleasant guitarist.

[2] Company reports are now so elaborate that some companies offer shareholders a concise version containing the legally required information; one wonders whether more than one in a hundred shareholders reads right through a company report.

[3] The growth in staff numbers from less than 1,000 in 1939 to more than 1,800 at peak about the year 1980 could not have been handled without computerisation.

pension fund as one of their trustees, continuing until his retirement in 1986. He is now one of Arnotts' longest-serving senior staff. Paul Weber succeeded him as trustee.

The largest single office before and after the Second World War was the wholesale office. It contained not only the clerks dealing with wholesale customers' accounts but also the packing room, staffed by members of the Irish Transport and General Workers' Union. It had been managed by Leslie Montgomery until his appointment as company secretary. It was then taken over by Jim Lyons. Since most of the wholesale goods were delivered by lug rail, served by two open lorries plying from the parcel office at the top of Prince's Street, the work of packing needed a large staff. Pre-war, packers were paid 65s instead of the porters' rate of 62s 6d – to become a packer was one of the opportunities for promotion of members of the ITGWU.

The rate for delivery by lug rail did not allow for the bulking of separately boxed or wrapped items. It was necessary, therefore, to assemble all goods ordered by each wholesale customer so that these could be included in one large packing case. Each packer had a 'station' which was a low platform to which the goods he had to pack were brought by lift and trolley (and after the rebuilding of 7–10 Henry Street miraculously by chute from all the upper floors). Packing was an art and ex-soldier Jim Lyons was very proud of the men under his command. During the First World War he had once been buried; his gruff manner made Arnotts staff wish at times that he been left buried.

Lyons was also very proud of the invoices typed on the NCR machines recommended by the auditors in 1956 which cost £2,323 each. The operators produced long sheets of invoices of which copies were filed in special binders in solid slabs. From month to month Lyons carried these binders up to the chairman's room to be admired. Before Craig Gardners' intervention long, plainly ruled and perforated duplicate books were used in wholesale departments to produce charge dockets listing and pricing the goods sold. Totals were calculated by the group of comptometer operators under the command of Jane

Kerrigan. The use of comptometers added a higher scale of pay in the offices and was partly responsible for office staff achieving a degree of parity with the sales staff. Sales staff were originally paid more as the 'earners' of the drapery trade, with commission usually added in the larger shops.

In the end, computerisation superseded the ledger posting machines. John O'Sullivan later had considerable trouble persuading the wholesale buyers and office staff that, if the charge books handwritten in the departments were carefully designed and clearly written in triplicate, it would be possible to produce with little further work a packing docket, an invoice and a record of the departmental sale. When CIE allowed separate packets consigned in one delivery to be charged at bulk rate, there was no further need for the extensive packing room.

Instead, Jim Hughes as wholesale director, moved the packers into the departments so that they, like the sales staff, worked directly for the department managers. This was at first suspected of being wasteful of manpower. What if one department had too much work for one man and another too little? This did not happen, partly because packaging developed at the manufacturing stage so as to minimise the work at the wholesale stage, but also because the work of selling set the pace for the department packer as a member of the team; he in turn responded to the needs of his department.

Earlier records of wholesale trading by Arnotts show that control of credit caused problems, and failures were common enough. The firm principle was developed that, in the granting of credit, the office manager, retail as well as wholesale, was answerable only to the chief executive; he could not be overruled by any general or department manager in the interest of making sales. Wholesale credit, being relatively larger in amount and not so spread as retail credit, was riskier.

Paul Weber has just retired after nineteen years' guardianship of Arnotts' rapidly increasing retail credit, strongly supported by June O'Brien and Carmel Barry and backed by the computer. Neither Weber nor Michael McGinn, who managed the wholesale office from 1977 until his very 'tidy' closure of the wholesale accounts, had to give way to sales managers in the opening or control of credit.

The change during this century in the sale of goods on credit has been profound, from long term credit without charge for the favoured few to universal credit with heavy charges 'sold' freely by financial institutions to anyone whose regular earnings hold out promise of consistent monthly repayments.[4]

The test of creditworthiness in the 1930s was that of ultimate payment. In those days 'Please pay' stickers for attaching to statements were available in a range of colours running up through yellow to red in tones that became increasingly peremptory. One suspects that this treatment merely innoculated the debtor against prompt payment. One woman of substantial means admitted that she bought household goods in Arnotts' Sale and did not pay for them until red stickers appeared on the statement of account as the next Sale was approaching.

With rising inflation, the patient approach of Joseph Byrne until 1963, followed by kindly Leslie Worrall until he replaced George Towers as chief cashier in 1974, was seen by John O'Sullivan to be out of date, and a stronger line with over-stretched retail credit was taken. This caused some frightful indignation, with appeals to directors. For some time we wondered if the tough new policy could be sustained.

The introduction of Arnotts' budget accounts had brought an influx of young women clerks, alarmingly called 'credit controllers', to the retail office; they may have lacked the gravitas of the older men.

In ordering a computer Arnotts had realised that it was indeed a strange new pet and needed not only to be fed, but actually taught to behave. Michael O'Toole, who was chosen from the counting house to become manager of its team of keepers, on his retirement left a detailed archive of its education. The remaining members of this team include

---

[4]Competition between lending institutions is now causing over-lending to a crazy extent. Ill health or unemployment can bring an edifice of debt tumbling down.

George Towers, the chief cashier, (right) with colleagues in the cash desk on the ground floor

(from left) Jim Riordan, Andrew McGorlick, John Collier, John Carty and Tommy Lonergan at Howth 1953

Desmond Ormonde, systems analyst, who had to decide on its curriculum, Blanaid Tuomey who, as programmer, had to provide it with the necessary instructions, and Pat O'Neill who had to feed and care for it day by day. To make things more difficult the newcomer was not approved of by the staff generally; it was very easy to make it a scapegoat for mistakes, and full advantage was taken of its vulnerability. Michael O'Toole had the exact temperament, patient and detail-tolerant, for this work. He did not flinch. It was Leslie Worrall, retail office manager, who declared: 'In the late 1960s I recall my most traumatic experience when we changed over to computer from NCR machines. It was quite hectic and exciting to be sure. I shall never forget the atmosphere created at that period.'

The computer's first success was very definitely in the field of retail credit. It could calculate rapidly and accurately at the end of every month the charge due on accounts, revealing immediately the undercharging that had occurred until then. But of course the poor computer was blamed in its early days if any mistake was made such as charging to the wrong account. It is extraordinary how a long suburban street in Dublin will contain several residents with the same surname and almost identical initials. The inaccurate writing of addresses on bills, which caused wrong charging, was cured by the introduction of Arnotts' charge plate in the early 1960s.

By the time Paul Weber had taken over as manager of the retail office in 1974 it was clear that the old style monthly accounts had been completely outnumbered by the budget accounts. From that time, all new accounts were opened as free of charge unless outstanding on the 25th of the month following that of the purchases and the amount of credit was extended to twenty times any monthly payment that was arranged.

WORKROOMS IN ARNOTTS

Mrs Pearl Taylor started as one of the fitters handling the elaborate alterations to garments that were still common after the war. With her model gown workroom, she formed a very strong partnership with Elizabeth Heffernan, who moved in 1956 from the gloves department to buy model gowns. In 1965 this department was given the more up-to-date name of 'boutique' and catered for the top end of the dress trade with emphasis on Pearl Taylor's special making. It was a department of modest size which traded with consistent success and filled a useful niche at the top of the dress trade but was closed in 1973 with Elizabeth Heffernan's and Pearl Taylor's retirement. It is a sobering thought that after retirement Pearl Taylor refused ever to touch a needle again.

Mollie Green, in her hat workroom, was outstanding as a remodeller of hats for Winifred Gorry. In this most tricky of trades they were superb operators. Mollie Green retired in 1976.

Men's tailoring was the largest workroom supporting retail trade. The top floor was reserved for it in the rebuilding of 7–10 Henry Street in 1960. It was directly above and therefore of the same size as the shirt factory below. With the support of department manager, John O'Reilly, and the management of Sam O'Halloran (1953–1962) and Ted Rabbitt (1962–1988) with his assistant manager, Jimmy Mitten, it developed into a sizeable factory with the latest tailoring machinery and a staff of over a hundred. Its weekly output at peak was 160 pieces for stock and 90 made to measure, with 100 trousers added at one period. There were two measure cutters in the sales department as well as other stock cutters in the workroom. From 1970 onwards the measure cutters were in turn Joe Maguire, Dennis Redmond, Jim Corrigan and Martin Stapleton. In 1970, after eight years as a wholesale traveller for shirts and men's ready-to-wear, Anthony Nulty was persuaded by John O'Reilly that his future lay in retail tailoring. He has since been the cheerful and energetic epitome of salesmanship in that important area.

The carpet workroom was always on a generous scale. In the time of Tom Murray's buying, Arnotts, vying with Clerys, prided itself on having the largest staff of cutters and layers in Dublin. In the mid-1970s, Tom Murray became aware that some of Arnotts' men were working, out of hours, for Todd Burns. He brought two of them before the managing director to be severely reprimanded: Arnotts after all was paying all the expenses arising from their normal employment and did not expect them to exhaust themselves at premium rates outside hours.

Murray was quite dissatisfied with the strength of the reprimand delivered until the managing director suddenly said: 'If you work for yourselves we shall be happy to give you all the work you need to keep you busy. All we would ask of you is to pay your income tax.' Six months later two of the men decided to work for themselves. They were always waiting for Arnotts to open in the morning to get the work out for laying, and made much more money for themselves. These pioneers were followed in the end by all of the men except those few who were in charge of the stock and the cutting of carpets when the workroom moved to Dominick Street.

The remaining workrooms, for alterations to women's clothing, men's tailoring and curtain making, stayed in Henry Street since this provided close contact with the selling departments in executing customers orders. Harry Kenny has been managing the soft furnishing room and attending to customers' queries in this rather exacting end of the furnishing trade since 1958.

SERVICE STAFF IN ARNOTTS

The long-serving Bernard (Barney) Duff retired in 1969. Starting in the electric lighting engine room, and concentrating on the job of electrician after Arnotts went over to ESB supply in 1948, Duff could not possibly carry out all the electrical work needed for the developing factories and workrooms in the 1950s and 1960s. Instead he concentrated on rewiring the Henry Street store for the 220 ESB voltage, giving light where before was inadequate gloom and only the central daylight well had saved the day.

Barney Duff's son, Nick, was recruited to the customs clearance department which, under Jim Tallon and Cecil McGovern, was of critical importance in post-war trade, particularly in wholesale where quotas as well as tariffs complicated buying, but in return delivered into our hands a section of the trade too troublesome for smaller traders to undertake. Nick Duff specialised in the outdoor work entailing daily visits to Dublin docks.

In 1966 petite, industrious Nora Byrne retired from years of french polishing in Arnotts. Her father, Ned Byrne, was a gentlemanly and highly respected doorman for years. The doorman's uniform is worn now only on state occasions, by Billy McDonnell whose front of store role keeps him fully occupied.

In 1968 the trustees of Arnotts staff pension scheme decided to invite skilled maintenance men to join. Their earnings certainly suggested they should. This was the first move in a process of opening membership of the pension scheme to everyone employed by Arnotts. The closure in the 1970s and 1980s of most of the manu-facturing and workroom units removed numbers of young women who would not have been willing to join and whose average period of service was short.

The maintenance staff emerged at this period as an important group. They were often recruited after they had come to work in Arnotts for outside contractors. Jimmy Murphy and Jimmy Martin, who work to cabinet maker standards, joined from O'Connor and Bailey's. Another James Murphy (James to distinguish him from Jimmy), the storyteller of earlier chapters, was home-grown in Arnotts, having taken to machine maintenance. There were literally hundreds of sewing machines to keep in order in the work-rooms and factories and the newest of them were of increas-ing sophistication. James Murphy was elected staff trustee of the Alexander Fund which illustrates his standing among his fellow transport workers.

With Pat Fitzsimons and Colm Walsh as electricians, and the Edgely family, father and then son, Peter, to look after the steam boiler and low pressure heating systems, Arnotts was generally well-equipped to handle all daily maintenance.

In plumbing, an essential trade, and also in general maintenance, Joseph (Joe) Murphy, with his team, has become indispensable, as he is in his role as a comedian in Arnotts' Theatre Group – a latter-day George Robey. The theatre group had its origins in the early 1950s and was revived in 1980 by the enthusiasm of Betty Thompson, Bill Maher and Tony Larkin. With Marion Quirke as honorary secretary, the membership of the group is heading for a hundred.

In the 1960s, costs of maintenance began to rise noticeably. This was attributed to the maintenance men and the overtime they were often rather carelessly called to undertake. Investigation proved this theory wrong. The increase in cost was due to a concatenation of cleaners.

The senior cleaner was Mrs Sarah Keller, daughter of Mary Forrest who, in the 1920s and 1930s, fed William Nesbitt scrambled eggs and toast for lunch in a room on the first floor back along Prince's Street.[5] Sarah Keller declared it was difficult to find reliable women for cleaning. So, as the buildings in Henry Street developed, new cleaners were recruited. The trouble with the system was that each of them was given two or three pieces of work as it became available and each came to regard those as her 'property'. No reorganisation was attempted to make it easier for them to service their often scattered areas of responsibility. The result was that, unknown to top management, a large chain of cleaners had been built up, to which links were being added as required. In 1976, after Sarah Keller retired, Mrs Maura Keogh was recruited as forewoman under Charlie Dunne, and an efficient system with more developed washing machinery was organised.

While the wholesale division remained in Abbey Street/ Prince's Street there were large numbers of porters in the complex of buildings. With the maintenance men, they proved invaluable in emergencies. They sprang into action, as if the call was a test of their manhood, and needed little direction – they were in charge for once.

The author remembers one such time. In the late 1950s, he was standing in the women's suit department at the back of the store when something caused him to look towards the furniture balcony. Flames were leaping from a piece of furniture. He ran to the centre of the store for an

---

[5]This room was beside the recently uncovered stained-glass windows.

extinguisher where Martin Lawless was standing. 'Don't panic,' he said, 'there is a fire on the furniture balcony.' Surprisingly, Martin Lawless stamped round in two complete circles shouting 'Fire!' – not his usual type of behaviour. An extinguisher must have been played on the fire in less than sixty seconds but two sprinkler heads had already burst because the ceiling was low at that point. They put the fire out quickly but the water gradually flooded the floor of the balcony and started to seep through cracks to Tom Murray's carpet department below on the ground floor. All available porters and tradesmen hauled away and piled up the heavy carpet rolls until a mountain of carpets was out of reach of the dripping ceiling – a Herculean task.

The author cannot remember how long it took the fire brigade to certify that the fire was out and turn off the water, but the smoke had drifted across more than half the width of the store before it was realised that customers were still shopping on the other side of the retail floor; they had to be asked to leave. This account shows the effectiveness of manpower challenged by emergency, and the rapid dousing of fire by the sprinkler system.

During another fire crisis the transport workers in particular distinguished themselves since they were available after closing time. Billy McDonnell remembered: 'Arnotts had its tense moments in the 1970s. One night three incendiary devices went off at half-hourly intervals, after closing time. The linens, carpets and furniture departments were targeted but luckily the night staff were at hand and, with the sprinklers doing a splendid job, the fires were quickly extinguished.'

Certainly, in times of physical danger Arnotts' men, buoyed with the excitement of the moment, proved equal to the task.

14 CRESCENDO 1970–1981

AS NEW CHAIRMAN, Ronald Nesbitt was anxious to paint a full picture: his reports were six times as long as the last reports of the old chairman, in the first years at least.

It is very difficult for a chief executive or chairman to keep his fellow directors fully informed and more difficult still to boil all the detail down into a nourishing soup for the shareholders. Attention spans are relatively short and the world outside the company motors distractingly on in its increasingly noisy way.

Directors' Christmas meetings in the secretary's central first floor room overlooking Henry Street (a room swept away in 1992) reverberate in the author's memory; the 'comeallyes' of the carolling groups, the street traders' cries of 'last of the jumping monkeys' and the steady roar of the packed crowd made it almost unseasonable to take business *au grand sérieux*. In any case, Christmas trading plays so important a part in the year's results, and its outcome at that point is still so uncertain, that there was little that could be said beyond 'Happy Christmas'.

At this period there were six directors: three executives in daily contact, and three non-executive who were briefed frequently between the monthly meetings. The chairman had to check that the executive directors were *ad idem* and that the outside directors were fully informed. The overdue separation of the role of chairman from that of managing director in the 1980s brought the number to seven – a nice balance between the executives who might not see the wood for the trees and the non-executives who might see both the wood and the distant view.

Increasing awareness of inflation in the 1970s and the

gradual dismantling of import duties under the Anglo-Irish Free Trade Agreement tended to throw the trading picture out of its accustomed focus. The growth in national income, with the increase in exports achieved by new grant-aided industries, lent a rosy hue. Almost anything began to seem possible. Arnotts hoped to play a part in exporting in more than one of its manufacturing units, and did so in four of them for a while.

In welcoming the Minister for Industry and Commerce, Jack Lynch, to the opening of Irish Week in 1971, the chairman declared that 75 per cent of Arnotts' clothing trade was produced in the Republic. He looked forward to that proportion remaining substantial in conditions of free trade, though the White Paper of January 1972 presenting the case for accession to the EEC noted that jobs in clothing, textiles and footwear would be at risk.

Inflation was not really good for trade. It was good for sales figures, but expenses caught up rapidly. In 1972, the chairman reported to the annual general meeting that group sales had exceeded £10 million but that the greater part of the increase was a movement in the value of money rather than in goods. He continued:

> Of the resulting profits more has been drawn off in company taxation. This has cut into the amount available for reinvestment and development. Under the heading of reinvestment we have to consider the effects of inflation on our finances. Our stock, for example, must be rebought and a rate of inflation of 5 per cent would require an additional amount of £50,000 after tax in the year in rebuying our stock of about £1 million.
>
> Our retail stores continued to trade strongly during the year. Both Henry Street and Grafton Street secured increases of 15 per cent sales, and in Boyers the increase was 18 per cent; but on the other hand expenses rose more sharply in our retail division to counterbalance this. We are at the moment concentrating all our attention on Henry Street where a new roof level is being developed to

house our large furniture department; we plan at the same time to install escalators linking all floors, lower ground, ground, balcony and roof levels.

Our wholesale division too increased sales and its profitability has improved.

The departments based on manufacturing have moved ahead again. Both in wholesale and retail we are strong in men's clothing (our retail tailoring workroom was enlarged during the year) and we are planning further development of our shirt factory. At the end of the year, too, we moved our children's coat factory to a larger building in Dominick Street which we purchased for £55,000.

Our manufacturing subsidiaries have also increased sales during the year, very decisively in the case of Ballet Foundations Ltd which had a sales increase of 25 per cent of which over one quarter was exported.

This then was the crescendo of mercantile music at Arnotts in which all the members of our band joined. Away with the old fiddling! One could hardly play on too generous a scale. Government borrowing for investment in national development fuelled inflation. The tempo increased.

In 1973 Arnotts' report spoke again of inflation:

Trading in inflationary times is rather like climbing an escalator that is moving downwards. 7 per cent inflation requires us to provide, after tax, from our profits 7 per cent of the value of our net current assets to restore their position.

During the year in our main store in Henry Street we completed the new roof level. The new furniture department on our top floor must be the finest in this country. Our total selling space in Henry Street is now about 120,000 square feet. The rebuilding, under the guidance of our director, Michael O'Connor, was finished with a minimum of disturbance to our trading. We are proud of the final effect and particularly of the design of the six escalators which fit so harmoniously into our building. Our maintenance manager showed great resource during the whole operation and he and our suppliers performed an outstanding task in installing the escalators, two each night, over the Whit holiday weekend.[1]

In this period street organisations began in an informal way – in Henry Street primarily to arrange and pay for Christmas lighting. In this Arnotts took the lead, finding a ready response to a levy based on street frontage, measured by Michael O'Connor.

It proved more difficult to agree with Dublin Corporation that the street should be 'pedestrianised'. At first the self-elected committee of managers from Roches, Woolworths, McGivney's, Fitzpatrick's and Arnotts thought it would be unreasonable without a back entrance for every shop. Our hesitation may have allowed time for opinion to swing in favour; in the end only Mr Marks[2] declared he wanted his customers to be able to park their cars outside the door of his shop. In 1973 the street became traffic-free.

Between 1973 and 1984 the yearly inflation rate hovered between 10 and 20 per cent (except for the year 1978). In 1974 Arnotts' sales reached 15 million, an increase in two years of 50 per cent. But wholesale stock had doubled, partly due to rumours of coming shortages of material following ICI's disastrous explosion and fire at Flixborough. The ratio of stocks remaining at the end of 1974 to sales rose alarmingly in nine out of sixteen wholesale departments. They were buying not only garments but also materials in the piece for manufacturing.

To motivate buyers a bonus of 1 per cent of sales over a basic target had been introduced. Of course, sales are not everything, and it was clearly to be understood that an adequate gross profit and a satisfactory turn of stock were

---

[1] The maintenance manager was the redoubtable Charlie Dunne, but the escalators were not the first in our group – Boyers installed one several years earlier (in Ivan Hart's time) when we extended the first floor through to Cathedral Street.

[2] The privilege of switching on Henry Street's first Christmas lights was given to Mr Marks's son, because his name was Henry.

also required. In time of high inflation and apparently booming trade, buyers earned increasing bonuses, bringing their total pay in one or two cases above that of general managers. Moreover, as buyers were appointed group buyers responsible also for sales in Boyers of North Earl Street, Arnotts in Grafton Street and Melanie's in Henry Street, their earnings moved down as a percentage of trade towards the figure of 1 per cent in wholesale trading and towards or below 2 per cent in retail trading. This combination of increased earnings with lower percentage cost was attractive to all parties. If only it had been achieved with smaller stocks!

At Michael Nesbitt's suggestion, Melanie's was opened in 1974 in number 17 Henry Street. Arnotts was ground landlord and had taken possession. Melanie's traded profitably from the second year until in 1979 it was moved into 'rent free' space in the main store. The rent obtainable made number 17 an excellent investment for the staff pension fund; in 1993, number 17 is valued at more than four times its original cost. A branch of Melanie's also traded in Cork, until shortly before the Melanie trade moved back to Arnotts.

The main problem in trading is to sell without delay what one buys. Table 14.1 (overleaf) shows Arnotts' Henry Street sales, turns, expenses and profits at seven selected dates between 1948 and 1979.

It can be seen that the rate of money turn increased in retail rather than in wholesale trading. This was the achievement of nearly all our retail buyers, particularly of our women's clothing buyers, but also surprisingly of many of our men buyers of larger, traditionally slower-moving departments. This became of critical importance in times of high inflation. For example, in 1973 rising prices reduced the buying power of money in the Republic by about 10 per cent. With a money turn of ten in trading, 1 per cent of profits after tax was required to top up the money needed for restocking; the retail profit of about 4 per cent after tax was sufficient. But in wholesale a money turn of 4.8 called for over 2 per cent net profit after tax for restocking; this was more than the after tax profit of less

Table 14.1: Arnotts' Henry Street wholesale and retail sales, turn, expenses and profits 1948-1979

CPI	Year	Sales £000s		Money turn of stock		Gross profit %		Total expenses %		Net profit %	
		W	R	W	R	W	R	W	R	W	R
100	1948	1,368	1,012	3.7	5.7	10.4	20.6	7.0	10.9	3.4	9.7
119	1952	1,234	990	2.0	4.3	13.3	21.4	11.9	14.4	1.4	7.0
140	1957	1,401	1,012	4.9	4.9	13.8	25.8	12.5	15.4	1.3	10.4
147	1960	1,449	1,575	4.2	6.3	13.2	22.9	9.9	13.5	3.3	9.4
192	1967	2,369	3,684	5.3	7.5	15.9	24.0	12.4	14.3	3.5	9.7
308	1973	4,936	6,160	4.8	10.5	20.8	23.7	15.8	15.5	5.0	8.2
719	1979*	9,719	20,001	5.3	11.1	24.6	28.9	19.3	18.7	5.3	10.2

* without Robert Wallace Ltd

Notes:

1. 1948 was the first year in which the wholesale accounts were separated from the retail Henry Street accounts.
2. 1952 was a post-war dip which was not overcome in real terms until well into the 1960s. The consumer price index suggests 1948 sales should have doubled by 1967; at that date wholesale was still lagging slightly.
3. In 1973–4 oil prices quadrupled.
4. In 1978–79 oil prices trebled.

than 2 per cent. Plainly, money made in retail trade was beginning to sustain wholesale trading.

In his report to shareholders in 1975 the chairman spelt the message out clearly:

> It was always efficient, but it now becomes essential, to achieve higher rates of stockturn. This was not what we did in 1974 and the cost of carrying what proved to be unnecessary and wasteful stocks is reflected in our reduced net profit before tax. The year started with booming sales and like many other Irish companies we over-traded. The prolonged Dublin bus strike and the bombs in central Dublin [which killed more than thirty people]. . . left us struggling in conditions of mounting depression to reduce stocks to order.
>
> During the year we started trading as Allied Couriers in the business of securing and moving cash. This is a very natural extension of our retail

trade and being free from any effects of inflation promises well.

In 1977 the chairman had cause to widen his review to include social as well as monetary change.

Dealing with the effect of recent social changes such as equal pay for women, one-third of the difference between the scales in our trade was eliminated in the year to 15 January 1977 and the remaining two-thirds are being faced this year. And on 17 January we began our new year with a five-day working week for retail staff, rotating over six days of trading.

The achievement of six-day trading came store by store. Numerous meetings of store directors proved that all wanted it but none could agree on how to go about it. Arnotts had been steadily doing 12 per cent of its week's sales in Henry Street on Saturday until 1 p.m., and 35 per cent of its sales on Saturday full day in Boyers. It was therefore safe to guess that trade in Henry Street could be doubled on Saturday by remaining open until 5.30 p.m. – on every other weekday sales in the afternoon were double those in the morning. In fact, it turned out that Arnotts did 30 per cent of its weekly sales on Saturdays.

Saturday seemed to be the free day prized above all. It was already enjoyed by most of the office and factory workers. The deciding factor was unemployment in the drapery trade, which caused staff to consider the response that was required of them. One by one the majority of staff in each store voted for a rotating five-day week in return for a once-off payment. This rotation gives each employee a Saturday to Monday free weekend slightly more often than every six weeks, because of bank and other holidays.

In 1978 the long-dreaded rivalry between the distributive and the transport workers surfaced in acute form. At this peak time of inflation there were regular rounds of wage demands. On this occasion the Transport Union was the more pressing, and was bought off by the offer of £6 a week attendance bonus. The larger employers were the

Cutting shirts in the Robert Wallace factory. Design consultant and Terry O'Neill, head cutter.

James Fagan (left), Ronald Nesbitt and Michael O'Connor in conversation in the late 1970s

most affected by this settlement; the majority of smaller employers had few transport workers, and moreover had no desire to let this settlement affect their distributive staff.

Naturally the distributive workers, particularly the men in wholesale or retail drapery stores who did not earn commission to keep their earnings above those of transport workers, wanted an attendance bonus too. But the drapery branch of the FUE refused. A work-to-rule began. In Arnotts this was a pathetic affair, which management could regard only with irritated sympathy. It was clear that the distributive workers would not be satisfied with less than the same attendance bonus and it seemed quite unrealistic of the drapery branch to ignore this.

Seamus Duignan negotiated a productivity agreement which traded the £6 for items already being discussed by the drapery branch. The shortening of the lunch break to one hour and a clause expressing general agreement with flexible working were the main gains for the company. The week's work was fixed at five days of seven and a half hours, with three lunch breaks from 12-3 p.m. to leave the stores two-thirds staffed instead of half staffed in the middle of the day's trading.

Profits peaked in 1981 to £3.997 million before tax – five times greater than in 1970. Total sales were four and a half times greater, but the consumer price index had risen by four and one-third times. Instead of a triumphant race, at times it seemed more like a nightmare chase to catch an accelerating bus.

Through bonus share issues the ordinary capital had risen from £1.8 million to £8.7 million. This included two separate issues to staff, one in 1977 and the second in 1982, of 200,000 shares at £1; the first issue was doubled by the 1980 bonus making with the second issue 600,000 staff shares in all. In 1981, 1970 shareholders then had exactly 4.5 shares for every one eleven years earlier. Revenue reserves had risen by seven times and capital reserves, due to the first tentative realisation of the growing value of Arnotts' properties, by a more modest 3.4 times.

By 1981 sales in Boyers, North Earl Street, had reached £5.29 million from 27 departments. This was a fivefold increase on 1970's sales compared with a rise of 3.34 times in the consumer price index. A hotel in Marlborough Street had been bought and rebuilt to give an L shaped store with three levels in Marlborough Street as against two and a small lower ground floor in North Earl Street.

In retailing, our biggest traders were Con O'Shea, with his splendid floor of furniture, and John Golden, who was buying women's and children's shoes for our three stores, having handed over a substantial trade in men's shoes to Robert (Bob) Dollard. It was obvious that his had to be nick-named 'the golden group'. John Golden was immensely hard-working and successful; at least one Irish shoe manufacturer is reported as making sure he got a good night's sleep before showing Golden his range.

From Boyers James (Jim) Gibson graduated to buying linens for the group. He, too, is an exceptionally strong trader, and so good-natured he undertakes too much of the work himself – hardly a fault in our book. By this time, too, Joseph (Joe) McGann had handed over his splendid men's shirts and knitwear department to Daniel Conroy, and had ventured to organise a new sports department in our Liffey Street building. Our sports trade has, despite hiccups, been the best of our new developments in trading. Joe McGann was a wonderful selector of merchandise and a very patient and hard-working man. It is sad that his death came so early in his retirement.

In 1977, John O'Reilly's magnificent man's shop had been very ably taken over by his assistant manager, Peter O'Doherty. O'Doherty made only one mistake: despite repeated queries from general management he would not admit that the large tailoring workroom filling 7,000 square feet on the top floor of the new 7-10 Henry Street building, making at peak production 200 pieces a week, would swamp him when free trade was opening first English and later European supplies to him. At that stage the workroom had to become an independent factory to survive; import substitution was no longer enough. As a main supplier to our man's shop the output of men's suits was balanced by making three-quarters in ready-to-wear in a range of sizes, as against one-quarter in the more volatile made-to-measure. The result, partly from a decline in the made-to-measure trade, was that the workroom died gradually and became later a cooperative of limited size – still on the same floor with part of the up-to-date machinery. At the beginning of 1978 O'Doherty's buying could support the workroom and buy outside in the Republic and abroad, and as he became less able to support his workroom we must assume his good nature blinded him to the danger of over-production.

John O'Reilly's was another of Arnotts' families. His sister Pauline was a leading saleswoman in the women's shoe department. She had a talent for display which was just what we hoped to find in each fashion department since the display department could not be expected to cover all internal display work. John's daughter, Joanne, inherited his talent for management, successfully conducting the business of Boyers' attractive café until her marriage with Boyers' deputy manager, Brendan Roche.

John O'Reilly must also be credited with playing a part in staff training. He was more articulate than most and could convey to others the results of his own thinking. Rita Meares, who became buyer of the women's coat department in 1970, the sister department in a way of O'Reilly's man's shop, is said to have been greatly influenced by O'Reilly; to her credit she admits this. Rita Meares, thank goodness, is still our senior buyer of women's outerwear; her performance over twenty-three years has been impeccable, and her influence in staff relations on at least one critical occasion very positive indeed.

The inventive Winifred Gorry retired in mid-1975 and sadly died eighteen months later. Her fashion work was mainly taken up by Mary Tallon who was recruited from Brown Thomas in 1965 and graduated to buying in Margaret Kerrigan's department for scarves, handkerchiefs and lace, continuing the partnership with Tommy Lonergan, wholesale buyer, until his retirement in 1977. Mary Tallon is another fashion buyer always in complete control of her trading; she is capable of buying any of our largest women's clothing departments, but on several occasions has refused to change. We can only console ourselves for this lost opportunity by wondering who could have been found to replace her in the buying of the important bits and pieces – the height of fashion is often in these details.

We rarely find and successfully develop entirely new trading departments. Well before Majella Gleeson became lingerie buyer she had proved herself to be the most versatile and useful buyer. As we have seen, she began by turning the old Berlin's department into a successful niche trade in homecrafts. In 1958 she started a new gift department aimed particularly at the trade in wedding presents, and two and a half years later combined it with the ailing department selling china and household goods. Sales climbed from £55,000 to £139,000 in the ten years to 1970. The consumer price index rose by a little more than half in the same period. One of her unusual experiments was with candles and other goods specially intended for sale at Christmas. Copenhagan and Frankfurt were the sources for candles. Arriving in Copenhagen with red candles in mind, she found that the Danes used only white candles at Christmas, though they could supply a whole gamut of colours. Working over her orders in her hotel in the evening Majella Gleeson decided to buy half her candles in red and the rest in descending number in white and other colours. Reordering was largely in red because Arnotts customers bought 90 per cent in red.

Finally, in our retail trade we were proud of our success in boys' and girls' clothing and school uniforms. In 1960 Michael O'Dwyer left the men's knitwear department to Joe McGann and started to develop a boys' clothing department from a trade hitherto carried on by John O'Reilly. In the first twelve months sales in Henry Street were £50,000; by 1981 sales had grown to over £1 million including sales in Grafton Street and Boyers.

Eileen O'Driscoll followed Mary McGovern in 1966 as buyer of our girls' clothing, building that trade up from £130,000 in Henry Street to over £880,000 in the three stores. In 1972 Eileen O'Driscoll hived off a girls' school uniform department under the management of her assistant, Christina O'Donoghue, our expert in this rather special branch of the girls' trade. Our story here is incomplete without Miss Teresa Young, given special mention in dispatches by Campbell Heather as a very knowledgeable buyer of babywear. She ran our retail department for babywear from 1952 until her retirement in 1972. This infant's trade was then taken over by Eileen O'Driscoll until her retirement *cum laude* in 1989.

Even before Jim Hughes's appointment in 1958 as wholesale manager he was an outstanding figure in the wholesale drapery trade. Universally respected, popular in Arnotts and outside, he set out to build a competent trading organisation, devoting himself in the process to the detailed and constant review of all its activities. The separation of retail from wholesale concentrated the minds of our wholesale buyers on their task. Their number had dropped from a peak of eighteen in 1960 to sixteen in the early 1970s, again due to the abandonment of trade in piece goods in favour of trade in garments. Only two buyers, Cummins and Lonergan, remained from twenty years earlier, the period of post-war boom, but as many as ten had been in place before 1960. Newcomers included Ross Dallas for children's coats, Peadar Farrell for hosiery, Ciaran Gannon for the shirt factory, Thomas (Tom) Tunney for men's readymade clothing – altogether a stable and experienced team.

The most notable change was in the selling organisation. Pre-war there had been five general country travellers supported by buyers or senior staff selling from stock-rooms or on special journeys usually at the beginning of spring and autumn seasons. In 1955 there were more than a dozen regular travellers and by 1970 there were nineteen. The newcomers had taken over parts of the very large range carried originally by the general travellers in heavy vans with a special driver; now all travellers had lighter vans chosen as suitable for the samples they were carrying. In the end, a number of them had saloon cars which were more comfortable and not unsuitable for lighter goods. It also seemed sensible to ask those selling in more remote areas to live in their district; Clement Hallinan lived in Cork, William Byrne in Galway, Anthony McGinty lived in Donegal up to 1967.

The additional travellers usually specialised, 'carrying' a related group of goods, for example, men's clothing or women's clothing. There were over a thousand outlets in the Republic for this wholesale trade and Arnotts seems to have dealt with nearly all of them at one time or another. Over time the trend was from 'general' trade into specialising in men's or women's and children's trade.

This promised well for our departments which had factory units, the shirt factory, the children's coat factory, or the commissioning of garments made from materials bought specially by Arnotts. In 1974, six wholesale departments had stocks of materials at cost for making up totalling over £500,000. This dragged their money turns of stock in that year down below 3, an impossible figure with inflation for the year at 17 per cent.

The wholesale trade admittedly had a certain dash about it that was not so obvious in retailing. A quietly dashing wholesale buyer in Arnotts was Tom Tunney. Taking over our men's readymades department in 1966, by 1972 he had increased its trade by 2.5 times, more than twice the rate of inflation. A large part of that trade was men's trousers made with unusual South American materials and a permanent pleating system called 'Corotron'.

Tunney was once worried about the financial stability of one manufacturer. £50,000 of Arnotts' material was in the factory and payments by Arnotts for cut, make and trim were in advance of delivery. The author accepted a lift in Tom Tunney's Ford car to look at the factory and talk to the manufacturer. At that time Tunney was only allowed business expenses on his car – it was not until 1975 that Arnotts provided cars for executive directors and other managers. The manufacturer had his expensive car standing outside. Tom Tunney's sly smile was as unforgettable as his good humour at the contrast between his lifestyle as the 'employer' and the man he was financing to make goods for Arnotts. We decided to continue support for three months, after which stocks of our material on the supplier's premises was to be limited to two weeks' usage; we wanted the trousers which sold like hot cakes. They were among the first readymade men's trousers we had seen that fitted a slim figure without hanging down at the seat like a sack. We got all our goods safely in the end. This trade in men's trousers was probably typical of the sort of specialisation on which our wholesale trade should have concentrated in the 1980s. Instead, we remained spread into men's suits, at a time when more casual garments were gaining ground.

In 1964, Peadar Farrell took over the hosiery department, that great perennial of the drapery trade, on the retirement of Paddy O'Flaherty. He did not inherit the retail stockings department; thus was broken the last link between wholesale and retail buying. Peadar Farrell distinguished himself and Arnotts by becoming President of the Distributive Workers' Union. During his presidency a delegation of trade union officials visited Dublin from the Soviet Union. Peadar Farrell's counterpart was a woman; a very suitable sex to represent Soviet distributive workers but the cause of some amused comment at the time in Arnotts.

As early as 1959 Samuel (Sam) Poole came to Arnotts to buy Jim Hughes's wholesale drapery department (cotton piece-goods). Inheriting a trade of £150,000, by 1981 he had increased it to very nearly £1 million. In addition, in 1976 he took over Hugh Neary's old department called 'flannels' from Tom Walsh. Sam Poole was an unusually quiet and serious man; probably for that reason he was chosen by the members of the staff pension fund to represent them as trustee from 1969 until his retirement.

The other members of our wholesale buying team were Edward (Eddie) Keogh, appointed buyer of women's knitwear, blouses and skirts in 1955 and Robert (Bob) Ruske who bought women's underclothing from 1959.

Thomas Kinsley, who had been buying women's coats, suits and dresses since 1956, was asked in the mid-1970s to reorganise our wholesale trimmings and millinery departments. On the retirement of Tommy Lonergan he also took over his neckwear. This was a wide remit intended to simplify administration at a time when the wholesale was under pressure. Tommy Kinsley's changed role created an opening for the recruitment in 1976 of John Connolly as buyer of women's coats, suits and dress. The hope again was that the future of wholesale also lay in trading up; this department promised and performed reasonably, but no breakthrough for the future was achieved on this front.

In 1977 the wholesale shirt factory became a subsidiary, Robert Wallace Ltd., called after that outstanding chairman of Arnotts in the earliest years of the century. When Ballet International moved from Dominick Street to its new factory in the Dublin Industrial Estate near Glasnevin, Robert Wallace Ltd. took up the vacant space and moved out of the upper floor in Henry Street. The success of Ballet International led us to hope that another of our units could stand on its own feet. This final investment in shirt manufacturing was perhaps an act of filial piety towards William Nesbitt who died in 1978 two months short of his ninety-fifth birthday. He had set such store by manufacturing.

While Derek Connerton was manager (he had spent his first years in Arnotts retail and in 1973 graduated to management of our wholesale shirt trade and factory) new machinery, particularly for collar-making, was bought. A trade had been developed in Ireland under the 'Robert Wallace' and 'Robbie' names, but after Derek Connerton resigned to go into business on his own account we failed to find the management needed to avoid running into losses. The factory was closed in 1983. Founded in 1912, many women had been employed in it for part or all of their working lives.

In 1977 the Merrymaid factory for children's coats was closed; it had not succeeded in maintaining its original up-market trade despite the enthusiasm of its young manager, Ray Winterson. Two years before this, a meeting of Arnotts' directors suggested that the group's activities should be more concentrated on trading and involvement in manufacturing reduced. For that reason also it was decided, in August 1987, to close Milne Models when its last manager, Senan Moloney, died in service. Miss Lily Carty, his lively and generously built manageress, tidied up this business, which had run with modest but real success since the 1930s, and took her retirement. In all these closures older staff were pensioned and younger staff were awarded redundancy payments, usually at quite a multiple of the statutory benefit.

Senan Moloney was a wholesale traveller turned manufacturer. A quiet, tall, bespectacled man, he was popular with everyone from staff to managing director. This probably saved his bacon when his passion for golfing led him to park his company van on Sandymount Strand one evening while he practised his other type of driving. The incoming tide surprised him and engulfed the van. The fact that the van seemed little worse for the experience may also have mitigated his sentence.

In March 1979, the author retired as managing director and his son Michael was appointed in his place. Michael Nesbitt started in Arnotts, Henry Street in Autumn 1968, attached at first to John Doody, retail manager and after that to Jim Hughes, manager of Arnotts wholesale. In 1972 he was appointed manager of Arnotts in Grafton Street and in the following year replaced Leslie Montgomery as a director of Arnotts. In December 1973 he moved to take over direction of Boyers with Seamus Duignan as his general manager.

Jim Hughes also retired in 1979 as wholesale manager and was replaced by Brian Howard who had, after some years as ADM with Eddie Keogh in the wholesale department for women's blouses, knitwear and skirts, become wholesale sales manager.

Ivan Hart, who had managed the initial build up in Boyers, unfortunately decided to leave us at the end of 1973. He left behind him an organised and well-disposed staff into which the group buyers from Henry Street had been smoothly integrated. It was indeed noticeable how assiduously buyers like Michael O'Dwyer, to name only one, had set out to cater for Boyers. It was a short walk from Henry Street and the removal of Nelson's Pillar, unplanned by Arnotts, had brought the sister stores a little closer. With Seamus Duignan as general manager and from 1979, on Michael Nesbitt's proposal, as managing director of Boyers Ltd, a very steady control of expenses was maintained, building profits into second place after Henry Street.

The management of Arnotts in Grafton Street was taken over in 1974 by William (Bill) Kelly who had come to the notice of John Doody. In the man's shop in Henry Street he showed unusual talent for promotions combined with a strong feeling for security. It must be true to say that Doody's mantle fell on Bill Kelly. By 1981, Grafton Street trade was £3.45 million with 21 departments in a building extended by the purchase of number 104; that figure was just short of seven times the sales in 1970.

The assistant manager to Bill Kelly in Grafton Street was Marie O'Rorke. Starting in Arnotts as a trainee, Marie O'Rorke became buyer of knitting wools in 1962 and in 1969 took over the glove department in Henry Street. Her attractive personality, particularly her sympathetic manner, qualified her naturally to be the face which management wished to present in Grafton Street. While there she played a large part in developing the Christmas party for retired members of Arnotts staff; this was later moved to Henry Street.

John Doody became deputy managing director of Arnotts in 1979; as far as retail trading was concerned he had occupied this position in Henry Street since 1972 when Vivian Dudgeon moved from managing Grafton Street to be his sales manager. In 1981, John Doody retired and resigned his directorship promptly to live in his idyllic Killarney. Vivian Dudgeon became general manager of Arnotts retail and was coopted a director of Arnotts in John Doody's place.

This chapter ends with the year 1981 which shone at the time as a financial highlight though overshadowed by the threat of a very high rate of value added tax (VAT) of 18 per cent on clothing and footwear. This was removed by the narrow defeat of the Fitzgerald coalition government. The chairman's statement in early 1982 concluded:

> The remaining uncertainty for 1982 consists precisely in that burdening and stagnation of our economy, and of the economy of the western world, which at the moment, apart from a short-lived pre-budget boom, is holding the rate of our increase in sales down to less than the obvious continuing rate of inflation. During this period we shall be moving the stocks of our wholesale division into our new

warehouse, not, of course, without costs both foreseen and unforeseen; and we cannot yet say that our factories have run into favourable conditions. Space will be freed for retail department store development, but the benefit from this will not be immediate. With ever rising expenses and less than buoyant sales we must then still regard 1982 as a year of uncertainty. Our management and staff proved, however, in 1981 that they could ride the poor conditions of last year and we are confident they will give a reasonable account of themselves in whatever conditions 1982 brings.

Arnotts in the 1980s, showing the pedestrianised Henry Street

15 *RECULER POUR MIEUX SAUTER* 1982-1993

THE STATEMENT BY the chairman to the annual general meeting of May 1982 struck a sober but not a despondent note. Profits before tax had peaked in 1981 and it was possible to think Arnotts would do as well in 1982.

It was still hoped that Robert Wallace Ltd would prove to be as successful in manufacturing shirts as Ballet International Ltd was with women's bras and underwear. Ballet's heavy dependence on sales to multiple retailers, in which the loss of any one customer would be a severe setback, was a concern. But, as we have seen, in autumn 1980 the minority interest of Gossard Holdings in Ballet International was rebought for £450,000 and sales of own brands in the United Kingdom were being developed and other countries explored for export trade.

With hindsight it can be seen more clearly that plans for the wholesale trade had the effect of putting it finally to the test. The bulk of its trade loomed large from Prince's Street to Abbey Street and inhibited profitable retail development. The space actually occupied by the whole-sale trading departments was between 30,000 and 40,000 square feet, so, including space for receipt and dispatch of goods, it was not unreasonable to plan a new warehouse of 60,000 square feet. The original idea was to retain the trading function, buying and selling from sample, in Abbey Street with traveller representatives reporting there as before; the bulk of goods would, however, be delivered to a purpose-built warehouse and bulk deliveries made from there.

The wholesale trade had developed as a wholesale department store, somewhat on the pattern of the retail:

their accounts were separated as late as 1948. With expenses rising strongly, the directors of Arnotts now realised that its operation must be streamlined, computerised and as highly automated as possible. Some progress had been made in the packing of goods in the quantities normally handled by retail shops so that the old time-wasting breaking of bulk quantities could be avoided. The development of branded goods helped to standardise qualities in greatest demand. It was clear, however, that there was still a long way to go before an efficient warehouse was developed.

The times were not on Arnotts' side. The rising consumer price index in the early 1980s, and the increases in salaries of managers used as a headline for increases to staff which followed them, evoked particular comment in minutes of directors' meetings from John Doody and later Vivian Dudgeon. Increases of 12 per cent for two years running could not be carried by an increase of 7 per cent in retail sales in 1982; profits before tax were hit where it hurt most. Arnotts did not recover until the end of the 1980s.

That recovery was not achieved without calling for considerable redundancies and early retirements among the staff. This had been anathema to management in Arnotts in the past, which took pride in providing employment and it was resisted to the last moment. It seemed careless to have overstaffed and so make redundancies inevitable. One felt compassion for those of middle age, falling between the insouciance of youth and the security of a pension.

In 1982, most of the wholesale staff moved to the new 60,000 square feet single-storey warehouse just beyond the junction of the Long Mile Road with the Naas Road. The transport staff took this move hardest and a small bus had to be provided to ferry some of them from central Dublin daily.

In preparing for the change we had satisfied ourselves that sales to wholesale customers visiting the wholesale departments were in almost every case a very minor proportion of the whole. The bulk of sales were made by the travellers from samples, not over the counter by sales staff as in retailing; the lower wholesale margins could not cover this additional service. The position of the new warehouse seemed convenient enough for most wholesale customers visiting Dublin by car, particularly for the more substantial traders.

An early trouble in 1982, arising from the new separation of the wholesale buyers and salespeople from the bulk of stock handling, was a critical shortage of telephone lines between Abbey Street and Naas Road. An agitation by wholesale management began for a complete transfer to Naas Road and by September 1982 the chairman is recorded in directors' minutes as speaking in favour of this for reasons of economy.

This was probably the critical mistake. The new warehouse might have been left to start swimming or to sink, rather than taking the heart and the rest of the brains of the wholesale business out of Abbey Street. In 1982, wholesale profits before tax dropped to £66,000. Sales were lower by less than 5 per cent and gross profits by less than 2 per cent but stocks had risen by 32 per cent, markdowns had doubled and increased overheads had wiped out any hope of satisfactory net profits in that year. The over-optimistic target set for sales had been missed by as much as 16 per cent, a full half of the additional stock having been bought to meet those larger sales.

Despite the wholesale shirt trade's separation into the subsidiary Robert Wallace Ltd, other wholesale sales had continued to increase in 1980 and 1981, but after the near 5 per cent fall in 1982 they fell again in 1983, this time by over 10 per cent. This fall was spread fairly evenly over the fifteen departments. Moving the entire wholesale business to Naas Road, with the increase in expense and marginal loss of sales which that involved, had reversed the earlier years' achievement of a modest rate of net profit before tax of 5 per cent into a loss of the same amount (£502,000).

It would be unfair to blame all of this on Arnotts' management because the drapery trade as a whole was depressed and in May of that year Robert Wallace Ltd felt compelled to reduce its planned production from 350 dozen a week to 150 dozen of higher quality.

In January 1985, Jim Hughes resigned as director of

Arnotts plc.[1] This was effectively the end of his influence on the wholesale division. Joan Lawler of Ballet International, who had been coopted to Arnotts board in Hughes's place, was invited to chair a 'think tank' including Brian Howard, wholesale manager, Derek Browne, accountant on special assignment to wholesale, Maeve Kenny, wholesale promotions manager and Jim Power, general manager in Ballet International. After an interim report brought useful savings in expense such as changing the over-developed delivery system, the group's final report suggested separate development of two main areas, women's clothing and men's clothing. Under buyers John Connolly and Berrie Stronge, who had succeeded Tom Tunney, both areas of trading had shown a notable increase, particularly men's clothing, but, with inadequate stock turns and heavy mark-downs at times, neither department could in the end save the wholesale division. By 1985, the number of wholesale departments had been reduced effectively to eight, which was exactly half the number trading in 1979. This reduction was achieved by the amalgamation of related areas of trading as buyers retired.

In 1985, sales increased by 11 per cent and, with an improvement in the overstocked position of the year before, a small profit was made despite heavier mark-downs and discrepancies. In 1986, sales were steady and a reduction in overheads following the Lawler reforms gave a wholesale profit before tax of £216,000. With this encouragement, wholesale persevered for two more years with profits before tax of just over £100,000 in each year.

The Lawler report could not recommend any course of action for the 'odd' departments: underwear, carried on reliably as ever and even at a small profit by Bob Ruske; trimmings in the same way without loss by Tommy Kinsley, and, *mirabile dictu*, the out-of-esteem household/piece goods department, bought by a younger buyer Maurice Connolly, which, in the last two years of wholesale trading,

---

[1]The company had been renamed under the Companies (Amendment) Act of 1983.

At the Senior Staff Christmas Party 1992 (from left) Mary McCormack, May Kelland, Ella Nesbitt, and Nellie Hand singing their hearts out for Patrick Coffey at the microphone

(Left to right) Managing director Michael Nesbitt, Jacqueline O'Brien, Charles Haughey, Penny Nesbitt and Jacko Nesbitt at the opening of the exhibition 'Personal Recollections' at Arnotts, April 1990

1988 and 1989, actually showed 6 per cent net profit after meeting its share of overheads. Without support from all of the remaining departments the overheads became an impossible burden. It took courage and the clarity of mind of the new chairman, Tom Toner, to decide on closure at the end of 1989.

The staff in Arnotts wholesale had shown remarkably good humour and patience. In the last, very trying, period morale was surprisingly good. The collection of outstanding debts, always carefully managed by Michael McGinn and his assistants, Dymphna Grace and Kathleen Colclough, was completed very satisfactorily. Brian Howard, wholesale manager, retired at this time too, after staying on for six months to help in this task. The staff took advantage of new rules of retirement provided by Arnotts' strong pension fund, or accepted special redundancy payments, or moved to Henry Street to use their talents there. Among those who moved were Maeve Kenny, who joined Bill Kelly to manage sales promotions, and outstanding salesmen, like Michael Fitzmaurice, who, though he confesses to an initial nervousness, was most welcome in the linen department in Henry Street.

Quite apart from the sale of the warehouse off the Naas Road which as an investment fortunately just washed its face,[2] it was estimated that the closure of wholesale had freed up to £3 million for reinvestment in retailing. This was welcome; from 1984 Arnotts had ceased to run into credit at the bank every year in mid-January, as was formerly the rule except for short periods of years after unusually heavy investment. This was again achieved in 1990 and will continue to be pursued.

In January 1982, one of Arnotts' directors, James C. Fagan, suffered a stroke which greatly affected his speech. Some months later, after nominating Seamus Duignan, managing director of Boyers, as his substitute director of Arnotts, James Fagan resigned and sadly died the following year. Seamus Duignan was co-opted to the board in his place.

---

[2]The capital investment in building was realised with a modest increase to cover inflation.

James C. Fagan was a quiet, deeply religious man who could be relied on to take a moderate and sober stance in any crisis. He completely supported the prevailing view of Arnotts' directors that good relations with staff must be preserved, and on many occasions the management was grateful for his unwavering attitude. For years he lunched daily in Arnotts café on a diet of business talk and so understood and followed closely, without comment unless it was necessary, the workings of the business. A most valuable director: in many ways his mantle has fallen on Seamus Duignan, who shows the same quiet reserve. For some years Duignan acted for Arnotts in negotiations with house committees and trade unions with the idea of acquiring a special knowledge of this area.

Also in 1982, the directors of Arnotts plc were joined by Richard Nesbitt BL, as a first step in arrangements for the author's retirement from the board.

Back in Henry Street, management of retail trading had been difficult also for Vivian Dudgeon, retail manager and director since the end of 1981. In 1982 sales rose by over 7 per cent; total expenses by an almost unbelievable 25 per cent! But the guidelines for increases to staff for 1981 and 1982 had been of this order. This was the end of the period of severe inflation in which we wondered if our country was becoming a banana republic. Trade unions were quoting extraordinary figures as targets for increases in pay, and political parties were outbidding one another for power. Net profits in Henry Street alone dropped by £467,000.

In 1983, the rate of inflation fell to 10.4 per cent and retail sales in Henry Street increased by just 8 per cent. Direct expenses and overheads were fairly well contained after the extraordinary rise in the previous year; but it was of no help at all that the year ended, despite heavier mark-downs, with many stocks over budget. With an average money turn of 7 in each of those two years only the women's fashion departments and the beauty shop, at one end of the range, boys' wear and infants in the middle, and, altogether admirably, furniture under Con O'Shea at the heavy end, showed exemplary turns. Mai Bergin had bought for the beauty shops for the group since 1973 with determined control and success. It is an interesting department because such a large part of the stock is branded and many of the brands are 'represented' by special staff whose first concern is to sell their own brand.

Although most of the group buyers have been appointed from Henry Street, it would be quite wrong to give the impression that trading talent did not come from Arnotts' subsidiaries which in fact were a valuable source of staff. Among those who came from Boyers, besides Vivian Dudgeon and Seamus Duignan, are group buyers Jim Gibson, buying household linens, Ellen (Nellie) Carolan, knitting wools and haberdashery, Marie Quinn, lingerie at first and later girls' school uniforms, and Brian Gillivan who straightened out the difficult carpet trade in Henry Street. The latest buyer who grew to full stature in Boyers is John Sheil who had been ADM to a group of buyers from Henry Street in the development of men's trade in Boyers after the 1971 expansion. In 1986, he was appointed buyer of Boyers man's shop and in that autumn scored an immediate success with leather jackets, with sales of £43,000 worth in two days. In July 1989, he took over the buying of the sports department in Boyers and later the man's shop in Grafton Street and Stillorgan. In the same way, Joan Atley emerged as buyer of separates in Melanie's in 1977 and now buys that department for Boyers and for Grafton Street.

One of Vivian Dudgeon's first achievements as retail manager in Henry Street was to remove the backs from most of the display windows. Visually and psychologically this opened the store to the street, abolishing some of the 'stuffiness' of the typical department store.

Arnotts' display team, under Tony Mescall after the retirement of Harry Dillon, was greatly strengthened by the recruitment of women, of whom the earliest to arrive in 1963 was Marie Kearns. For window displays the acceptance of trousers as normal wear for women was timely. Our women achieved a more detailed use of matching accessories in the window displays of clothing and extended the areas of displays to strategic positions in the store as a whole. Kevin Byrne, who is now head of the display team, started in Grafton Street and, after Mescall left, took over in Henry Street. A lot of extra work is put into the exhibitions and other special shows by the display team, who now use a large section of the former tailoring workroom for their constructional work.

With the removal of wholesale from Abbey Street its ground floor became a bargain shop – a nice change from the usual bargain basement. This started with an overflow shoe department created by the quietly exuberant John Golden. Upper floors became special promotional areas, including the exhibition hall, and the reserve stockrooms were concentrated over the whole of the top floors along Prince's Street under the careful supervision of Tony Glennon.

The dictum of the fabulous department store man Gordon Selfridge, 'Give the lady what she wants', was rather narrowly interpreted by many store managers until after the Second World War. Good value and sterling worth were their guidelines; Arnotts had even questioned the morality of the cosmetic trade. Now we believe that shopping should also be entertainment, even theatre. With more space available in Henry Street we realized that the city centre had no obvious place for events or exhibitions. 'Where better that in Henry Street?' declared Bill Kelly, who had returned there in 1982. With 240,000 people passing Arnotts' front doors every day, he saw the opportunity of attracting them as shoppers by inviting them to visit all kinds of events instore. As sales manager he intended to adapt quickly to changing trends and topical issues.

Finding that Irish people loved meeting celebrities, particularly media and sporting personalities, he has given them many opportunities to do so.

When Joan Tighe of the *Evening Herald* came to interview a young and rising soccer star called Maradonna one of our beauty shop staff acted as Spanish interpreter; Arnotts made front page headlines in the *Herald* that evening.

In 1983, Dublin Captain Tommy Drum came in with the Sam Maguire Cup and some members of his team after the

Thomas C. Toner, chairman since 1986

When the Ireland-Russia football match was held in Moscow in
October 1985 Arnotts advertised in the stadium: Martyn Turner
remembers fears from the Cold War of silent Russian paratroopers
dropping from the skies over Ireland (courtesy Martyn Turner)

controversial final in which the Dubs finished with only twelve players, three having been sent off. An earlier All-Ireland medal winner with the Dubs was Kevin Moran, who, while playing for Arsenal, was the first player to be sent off the field in an FA Cup Final. Since the TV cameras showed this decision to be mistaken Kevin Moran was more than sympathetically received on his subsequent visit to Arnotts. Arnotts' sponsorship of the Dubs is a tribute not only to today's high-profile team and players but also to Arnotts' outstanding players of the past. Teams from Arnotts won the Kickham Cup for competition between Dublin business houses several times in the 1930s and 1950s.

This policy was a development of John Doody's cult of personality. To it Bill Kelly added the organisation of exhibitions, with Maeve Kenny's backing when the closure of wholesale freed her to return to Henry Street.

A large hall with pillars was now available for exhibitions. The idea of a Lego exhibition was introduced by Joe McGann, sports and toy buyer. Bill Kelly found that Lego had created touring exhibitions built with moving parts as educational models for children; they required 5–6,000 square feet of space. Arnotts' first Christmas exhibition, well-publicised by the press, attracted 295,000 people. This proved to be a world record for attendance at a Lego exhibition in relation to the size of the population. For Dublin's Millennium in 1988 a model of the City Hall was presented to the Lord Mayor, Carmencita Hederman.

Items as different as Japanese dolls and Soviet postage stamps have been exhibited. The invitation to show the stamps followed the unexpected cartoon in *The Irish Times* by Martyn Turner illustrated here. On impulse, we had put ARNOTTS SPORTS SHOP on a pitch-side hoarding for an Irish-Soviet soccer match in Moscow which had been very clearly seen on television by many viewers in Dublin.

Arnotts National Portrait Exhibition, which has been held each year since 1985, is our most prestigious event. With a committee of judges chaired by Robert Ballagh, the standard has been rising steadily: the work is adventurous and often technically astonishing.

Other exhibitions and promotions at Arnotts aim to be socially useful. One, printing a million Arnotts carrier bags with a message about the National Blood Transfusion Service, led to clinics being held in the store for customers and staff alike. In 1987, with Dublin Corporation Arnotts mounted an 'Age and Opportunity' exhibition to highlight the services available for retired people. Arnotts also provided space for runners in the *Evening Press* Women's Mini Marathon to register: 10,000 women came to do so and it developed into quite a social occasion.

Calendar 1984 was, by a whisker, one of the lowest points recently for profits before tax (£1.946 million). This was due to the full effect in that year of the introduction of VAT of 8 per cent on clothing (except children's) and of a higher rate of 23 per cent on household goods, in a year in which the increase in retail sales was only 4 per cent. In his statement to shareholders in early 1984, the chairman had pleaded for a uniform rate of 10 per cent to prevent distortions such as the initial tax of 23 per cent on a blanket and of only 8 per cent on that peculiar necessity, a bow tie!

Alterations in rates since then have brought this desirable uniformity a little nearer, but at a higher average level than in other EC countries.

The resulting lower gross profits and higher selling expenses had a crippling effect on group shops with smaller sales – Grafton Street and the Melanie branches in Dublin and Cork. The larger organisations withstood the shock better; indeed the effect on the smaller, which were concerned only with women's clothing, seemed relatively greater, as if women had immediately pulled their horns in for the benefit of their families. Retail management searched for economies. In 1984 two small departments had been closed following the retirement of their buyers and in 1985 a further eight were amalgamated with others. By the time of the author's retirement as director in 1986 a modest recovery in profits had been achieved.

This was not helped by the last major decision of his period as chairman, to merge Allied Couriers with the subsidiary in the Republic of the internationally known company, Brink's-Mat. Allied Couriers had been established and funded by Arnotts under the direction of the company secretary, John O'Sullivan, and the financial manager, Andrew Knowles. It had been managed very energetically and successfully by Owen Jones who had a 25 per cent stake in the business. Apart from a £50,000 capital loss in 1985, which was written off out of profits for that year, Allied Couriers had been a steady contributor of profits. After the merger, these profits almost vanished for a while. It is interesting to note that Owen Jones, whose retirement caused Arnotts to venture into the arms of Brink's-Mat, believed in moving coin, which was not of very great value, but was heavy and for the movement of which a relatively higher charge could be made, as against Brink's-Mat business of moving millions of pounds worth of paper currency. Recent changes in Brink's-Allied promise a return to the better days of Allied Couriers' youth.

In 1986, Arnotts was fortunate to find Thomas C. Toner willing to join the directorate and accept election as chairman of the company. His extensive experience of trading and his record of public service as President of the Federated Union of Employers suggested he was eminently equipped to oversee the reorientation of Arnotts into the 1990s. His energy, his interest in the peculiarities of department store trading and his firm financial grasp has established him more rapidly than most newcomers to our business.

In 1987, the search for economies continued. Closure of the tailoring workroom was discussed. Planned capital expenditure was frozen. By October, the sale of Ballet International to the acquisitive Crowther plc had been arranged; the imminent retirement of its creator Joan Lawler was a large factor in Arnotts' decision to concentrate on trading, abandoning manufacturing completely. On her retirement, Joan Lawler resigned from Arnotts board; her place was taken by Brian Davy of Davy Stockbrokers.

The cost of redundancies in the years 1985-1989 was considerable. In 1988, 50 were planned for Henry Street, but the total grew to 92, of which 10 were in Boyers. The movement out was unexpectedly popular. In many cases it was in fact early retirement facilitated by special rules adopted by the trustees of Arnotts' staff pension fund.

In 1984, Larry O'Dwyer retired and Blanaid Tuomey was appointed in his place as trustee of the pension fund; she had started in Arnotts' computer department and had also followed Larry O'Dwyer as head of the wages office. She had been a strong chairman of Arnotts' house committee and a trustee also of the IDATU.

In September 1988, after consideration of a consultant's report on the tailoring workroom that to survive it must become an independent manufacturing unit, we closed the workroom. A group of staff and tailors decided to carry on, tailoring for Arnotts with a loan of our machinery and space.

During the disturbed period of adjustment in the middle 1980s, even the careful management of Boyers under Seamus Duignan could not avoid the pressure of rising costs and the passing pain imposed by VAT. The Grafton Street store had also suffered severely in 1984 from the coming of VAT which caused stock reductions of 7.6 per cent of sales and wiped out profits. Recovery came in 1985, but the following year a steep increase in the rent of number 104 caused the withdrawal of children's and other departments from that part of the store. At that point, Grafton Street was re-planned as a store for women's and men's clothing under the name of the Fashion Gallery. The disruption of trade caused in refitting for this move had a disastrous effect, causing losses in 1988, but in 1989 an increase in sales of 11 per cent led to near break-even. Since then, a modest profit has been made in Grafton Street under the careful management of Mrs Dalton.

Rereading the statements to shareholders of the chairman, Tom Toner, from his first in 1988 to that of 1993, makes clear his grasp of the economic climate in which Arnotts has been operating. His second sentence in 1988 ran thus:

> As the government continues to act to restore the financial health of the economy, retail spending will remain depressed and Arnotts is acting to re-adjust the group's operations to regain and retain competitiveness. Substantial steps have already

been taken to reduce costs; in the current year the
objective is to upgrade the stores both in
appearance and the range of merchandise on offer.

Profits before tax had sunk again to £2.114 million after
an exceptional cost of £811,000 for redundancies. The
reaction of a William Nesbitt to stormy financial weather
would have been to batten down the hatches and reduce
investment to a minimum. But the terrible 1930s had not
quite returned and a courageous strengthening of the retail
stores could be financed by the sale, or closure at a cost, of
Arnotts' remaining manufacturing activities, and in
1989–90 of the wholesale division. The result was a steady
growth in profits before tax to a peak of £4.222 million
declared in 1992; at that date, too, year-end indebtedness
had been wiped from the balance sheet.

Much of the work of achieving this clearance of debt had
fallen on the company secretary, John O'Sullivan, who
retired in autumn 1990 after thirty creative years in
Arnotts. His final service was his constant support of
Andrew Knowles, who was appointed company secretary
in his place. Happily, John O'Sullivan continues as
secretary of Arnotts' pension fund which he has played so
large a part in promoting and developing.

In his statement of March 1992 the chairman was able to
report progress in all the stores and to add:

> Turning to future development, the major
> programme of reconstruction which I spoke about
> last year has begun in Henry Street. Building work
> will continue until the autumn of this year and
> when completed should improve further the
> appearance of the store, and provide additional
> retail space.

The completion of this ambitious project coincided with
a decided weakening in retail trade in 1992; Christmas
trade was particularly disappointing and interest rates on
renewed borrowing rose alarmingly with the depreciation
of sterling and the speculative attacks on the Irish pound.

The new octagonal dome was completed in time for the 150th anniversary celebrations in 1993

But the chairman reported confidently in March 1993:

> We are celebrating the completion of 150 years of
> successful trading with our major renovation of the
> Henry Street store. This programme, in addition to
> achieving a striking new interior to the main store,
> has increased the total retail space by some 20,000
> square feet and given new light and atmosphere to
> the store. The building work undoubtedly affected
> the level of trading but to a much greater extent
> profits suffered from the general reduction in the
> retail trade due to the currency crisis and very high
> interest rates in the second half of the year. In early
> 1993 we launched new departments and concession
> shops in the additional space which will add to our
> ranges of fashion and leisure wear. These, together
> with our enlarged furniture display, augur well for
> the future. In a first for Dublin, we have also
> opened a River Island Clothing Company shop
> which we are confident will be an outstanding
> success.

Michael Nesbitt had always admired the 'High Victorian'
character of Arnotts' 1890s building. He regretted the
removal of most of the cast iron capitals and other
Victoriana, for utilitarian reasons such as easier cleaning
and maintenance. In the 1992 reconstruction of the Henry
Street store the central well has been raised to the skies.
This has been the imaginative completion of the process,
started and so carefully developed by the O'Connor family,
father and son, of projecting the narrow balconies of the
original high-ceilinged single-storey retail floor. In stages,
purely for the sake of finding more floor space, they were
extended using the 'forest of pillars' for support; later the
back of the shop was built over, and finally, greatly daring,
the front.

In 1981, following the wholesale move to the Naas Road,
the work of raising the old ceiling along Prince's Street was
completed on time and on cost, with no disruption to the
existing business.

Ten years later, in Michael Nesbitt's time, the remaining

major surgery that the old building needed was carried out. Almost one hundred years after it had been built as a single storey high-ceilinged shop, lit by skylights, the raising of the ceilings in the remaining Henry Street frontage allowed the completion of the balcony level and the cutting away of the old roof to match a splendid octagonal dome.

Instead of a single storey shop, Arnotts now has a gallery of retailing floors with bright daylight flooding a large portion of the business core of the building. The whole is a splendid salute to 1993 and a statement of our confidence in the future.

Revaluations of Arnotts properties have been made at intervals in recent years. Long forgotten is the doctrine of Alexander and William Nesbitt that it was desirable to write these assets out of the balance sheet completely. The last revaluation published at the beginning of 1990 declared the properties at a total of £33.26 million and in that year a bonus issue of one £1 ordinary share for each ordinary share in issue doubled the ordinary capital to £17.4 million.

Our view of our stores is that they are naturally centres of shopping. The name Arnotts or Boyers is over the door and along the facia; inside, to our own trading departments, we are adding concession areas to introduce complementary goods, which make the whole more interesting and attractive to shoppers.

The shopping centres of today need 'anchor tenants' to pull in customers. Arnotts' trade in Arnotts' stores is the anchor which attracts other trading organisations to join us in continuing to develop outstanding centres of shopping.

ENVOI

GOOD SALESMANSHIP is a worthy profession; it can also be one of the more cheerful and rewarding. The leading professions are so often concerned with people who are sinning, or ailing, or angry and litigious, but salesmen and saleswomen deal with people in livelier mood – anxious perhaps, needing reassurance, but enjoying life and grateful for service. Selling is serving; surely another road to heaven.

APPENDIX:
FINANCIAL RESULTS

FINANCIAL information for the history of Arnotts is available in many long series, sometimes spanning the period from 1856 to the present day. Information is available by department revealing sales, stockturns and gross profits for the two sales seasons stretching back to the 1880s. General financial and balance sheet information is available over similar spans.

The graphs in the following pages have been chosen to show some of these long trends of data.

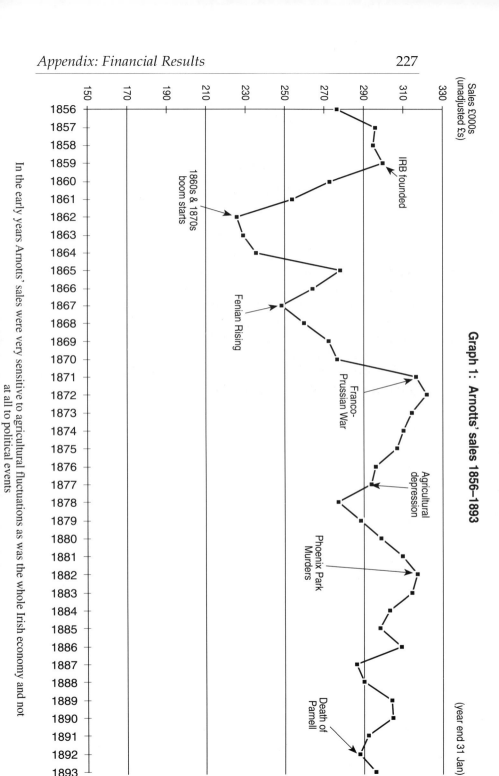

Graph 1: Arnotts' sales 1856–1893

(year end 31 Jan)

Sales £000s
(unadjusted £s)

IRB founded

1860s & 1870s
boom starts

Fenian Rising

Franco-
Prussian War

Agricultural
depression

Phoenix Park
Murders

Death of
Parnell

In the early years Arnotts' sales were very sensitive to agricultural fluctuations as was the whole Irish economy and not at all to political events

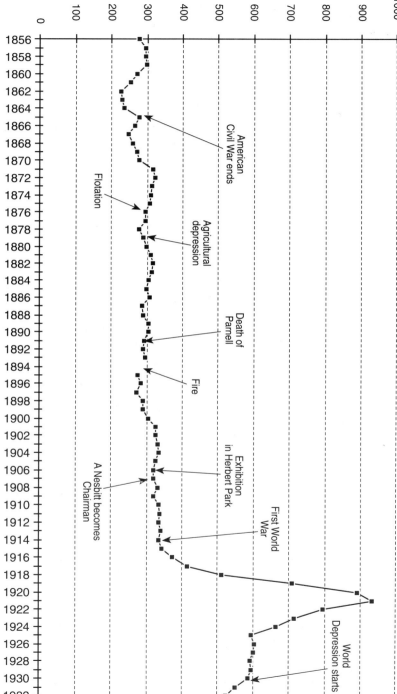

Graph 2: Arnotts' annual turnover 1856–1933

£000s
(unadjusted £s)

American
Civil War ends

Flotation

Agricultural
depression

Death of
Parnell

Fire

Exhibition
in Herbert Park

A Nesbitt becomes
Chairman

First World
War

World
Depression starts

By 1870 turnover had settled down at £300,000 a year, a level sustained in real terms (apart from the First World War) until 1940 (see Graph 3)

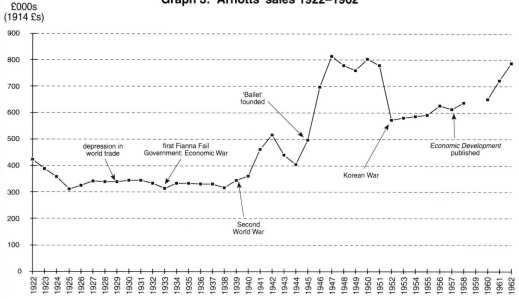

Graph 3: Arnotts' sales 1922–1962

£000s
(1914 £s)

Above: the Emergency period broke the pattern of sales permanently. Note how the contribution of manufacturing came into its own after 1945.

Below: the difficult years of the First World War destroyed long established patterns (see also Graph 5).

Graph 4: Arnotts' sales and profits 1909–1924

£000s
(unadjusted £s)

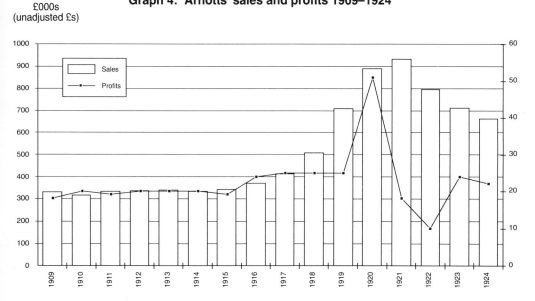

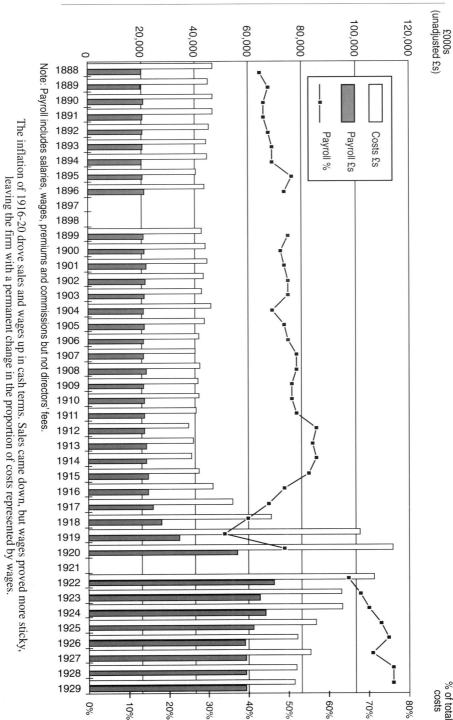

Graph 5: Arnotts' total costs and payroll 1888–1929

Note: Payroll includes salaries, wages, premiums and commissions but not directors' fees.

The inflation of 1916-20 drove sales and wages up in cash terms. Sales came down, but wages proved more sticky, leaving the firm with a permanent change in the proportion of costs represented by wages.

Graph 6: Arnotts' stockturns 1939 & 1973 in retail departments

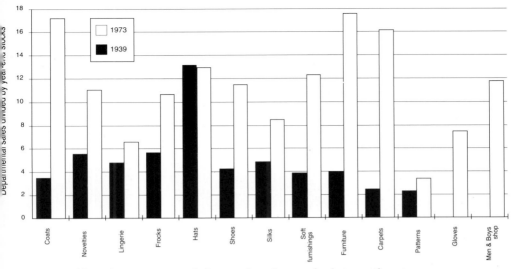

Many departments greatly increased stockturn ratios between these two years.

Graph 7: Arnotts' stockturns 1973–1987

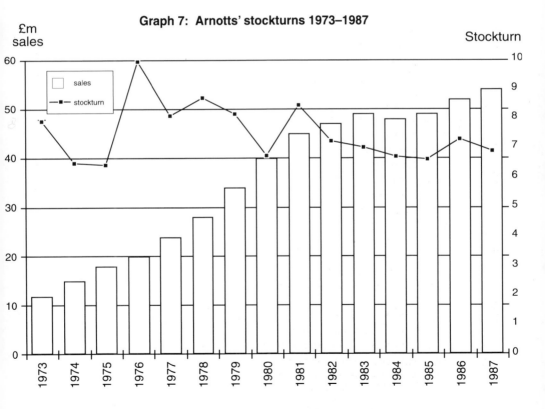

The inflation of the 1970s pushed sales to new levels; stockturn ratios changed little.

INDEX